EMOTIONAL PROBLEMS
OF AGING

EMOTIONAL PROBLEMS OF AGING

By

GEORGE THORMAN, M.A., M.S.W.

CHARLES C THOMAS • PUBLISHER
Springfield • Illinois • U.S.A.

Published and Distributed Throughout the World by

CHARLES C THOMAS • PUBLISHER
2600 South First Street
Springfield, Illinois 62794-9265

This book is protected by copyright. No part of
it may be reproduced in any manner without
written permission from the publisher.

© *1989 by* CHARLES C THOMAS • PUBLISHER

ISBN 0-398-05593-9

Library of Congress Catalog Card Number: 89-4556

With THOMAS BOOKS *careful attention is given to all details of manufacturing and design. It is the Publisher's desire to present books that are satisfactory as to their physical qualities and artistic possibilities and appropriate for their particular use.* THOMAS BOOKS *will be true to those laws of quality that assure a good name and good will.*

Printed in the United States of America
SC-R-3

Library of Congress Cataloging-in-Publication Data

Thorman, George.
    Emotional problems of aging / by George Thorman.
       p. cm.
    Includes bibliographies and index.
    ISBN 0-398-05593-9
     1. Aged—Mental health. 2. Aging—Psychological aspects.
3. Geriatric psychiatry. I. Title.
    [DNLM: 1. Aged—psychology. 2. Aging—psychology.
3. Psychotherapy—in old age. WT 150 T495e]
RC451.4.A5T47 1989
155.67—dc20
DNLM/DLC
for Library of Congress   89-4556
                                                                 CIP

PREFACE

Growing old in contemporary society imposes a heavy burden that many people are ill-prepared to meet. A gradual decline in physical and mental functioning and diminished ability to cope with problems take their toll as people age. The high rate of suicide among the elderly and the large number of older persons who succumb to mental illness leaves little doubt that emotional problems incapacitate many elderly Americans.

A growing interest in gerontology and a new attitude toward mental health treatment of the elderly are beginning to emerge. Psychiatrists, psychologists, social workers and gerontologists are providing a steady stream of information that emphasizes the importance of providing older persons with adequate professional services. Comprehensive evaluation of the emotional problems of older people and a genuine response to their needs are now accepted as worthwhile and important tasks. This new interest in the psychology of aging holds great promise for both older Americans and their families.

This handbook is designed to serve as a guide for psychologists, social workers, nurses and other mental health workers who serve the elderly and their families. It contains useful information for others who are called upon to aid older persons in the course of their duties as clergymen, physical therapists and hospital or nursing home administrators.

Chapter One provides an overview of the aging process and includes a description of the physiological, psychological and personality changes that are part of growing old and gives attention to the problems older persons face when sexual functioning changes. The problems associated with retirement from work and how individuals adjust to aging are also discussed.

Chapter Two describes the mental and emotional disorders that are associated with aging. The causes of these disorders and the various treatment methods employed to help patients cope with them are explained. The effect of stress as an important factor in dysfunctioning among older persons is also explored.

Chapter Three outlines the steps taken in making an assessment of the individual's emotional problems, including physical examination, a psychiatric evaluation, and study of the person's social environment.

Chapter Four describes social casework intervention in helping older persons cope with emotional problems, including supportive casework, task-centered practice and crisis intervention.

Chapter Five indicates how behavior modification, cognitive therapy, problem solving and integrative counseling are employed in working with older persons.

Chapter Six explores the use of family therapy and the family centered approach in helping the older person through an emotional crisis. The techniques of marital counseling and sex therapy are examined as they apply to working with older persons.

Chapter Seven introduces the group approach to working with the aged and includes a description of psychotherapeutic therapy, humanistic therapy, reminiscent therapy and assertion training.

Chapter Eight inquires into the various methods of treatment employed in long-term care and the problems associated with the relocation of aged individuals into institutional settings. Included is a description of hospice care and community health services designed to assist older persons.

Chapter Nine inquires into the emotional aspects of dying and death, grief and mourning and the ways in which the professional mental health worker can support older persons and their families face impending death.

As a practicing social worker, I have witnessed the heroic ways in which many older persons face the many problems that accompany aging. I hope that what I have written will provide greater insight into the nature of their emotional difficulties and point the way for helping America's senior citizens attain the quality of life which they so richly deserve.

George Thorman

CONTENTS

		Page
Preface		v
Chapter 1.	**The Aging Process: An Overview**	3
	Stereotypes about aging	3
	Physiological changes and aging	5
	Psychological changes	7
	Personality changes	8
	Sex and aging	10
	Adjustment to retirement	12
	Adaptation to aging	16
	Summary	19
Chapter 2.	**Mental and Emotional Disorders**	21
	Brain disease and neurological disorders	21
	Depression in late life	23
	Suicide	29
	Hypochondriasis	30
	Paranoid states	32
	Anxiety reactions	34
	Alcohol and drug abuse	35
	Sexual dysfunctioning	36
	Stress and aging	38
	Summary	41
Chapter 3.	**Assessing Emotional Problems**	43
	Conducting the assessment	43
	Physical examination	44

viii *Emotional Problems of Aging*

    Psychiatric evaluation................................50
    Assessing the social environment.....................53
    Planning intervention................................58
    A model assessment...................................58

Chapter 4. **Social Casework Intervention**............................61

    Supportive casework approach.........................61
    Task-centered casework practice......................67
    Crisis intervention..................................76
    Summary..87

Chapter 5. **Behavior Modification, Cognitive Therapy and Integrative Counseling**..........................89

    Behavior modification................................89
    Cognitive therapy....................................95
    Problem solving.....................................100
    Integrative counseling..............................102
    Summary...108

Chapter 6. **Family Therapy, Marital and Sex Therapy**...............111

    Family therapy......................................111
    Application and evaluation of family therapy........113
    Marital problems of older couples...................115
    The problem-solving approach to counseling..........118
    Sexual problems of older persons....................120
    Techniques of sex therapy...........................124
    Evaluation and summary..............................127

Chapter 7. **Working with Groups**..................................129

    Rationale of group therapy..........................131
    Group processes and interactions....................132
    Psychotherapeutic groups............................135
    Humanistic group therapy............................138
    Reminiscent therapy.................................140
    Assertion training..................................143

	Self-help groups	146
	Summary	147
Chapter 8.	**Long-Term Care for Older Persons**	149
	Assessment and decision making	149
	Relocation problems	150
	Therapeutic approaches	151
	Hospice programs	154
	Community mental health	156
Chapter 9.	**Coping with Death and Dying**	161
	Fear of death	161
	Emotional responses to dying	163
	Death with dignity	169
	Grief and mourning	173
	Learning to work with the dying	179
References		183
Index		187

EMOTIONAL PROBLEMS
OF AGING

Chapter 1

THE AGING PROCESS: AN OVERVIEW

There are now approximately 27 million persons age 65 or older in the United States. Aging persons make up almost 12 percent of the population and constitute the most rapidly growing segment of our society. Experts predict that one of every five Americans will have reached age 65 by 2030. Because more people are now expecting to live to an advanced age, there is a growing interest in the aging process and how it affects the lives of millions of our older citizens. Recent studies by physicians, psychologists, social workers and sociologists have thrown new light on all aspects of aging and challenged erroneous views of what it means to grow old.

Stereotypes and Myths

Shura Saul (1974) has identified certain stereotypes and myths that are still widely held: the myth of tranquility, the inevitability myth, the illness myth, senility myth, psychological myth, asexuality myth and the myth of unproductivity and family dissolution.

Tranquility Myth. Known as the "myth of the golden years," this extreme view overlooks the reality that old age is a time of substantial stress and that these stresses can lead to depression, anxiety, paranoia and psychosomatic illnesses that are associated with aging.

Inevitability Myth. This myth is based on a number of misconceptions. It assumes that all older persons are physically and mentally impaired and that the physical and psychological changes that come with aging are not only inevitable but that they are irreversible.

Senility Myth. This myth implies that all old people are "brain damaged," unable to think logically, are out of touch with reality and behave like children; it denies older persons of their right to dignity and worth.

Older People Are Not Treatable. This myth is based on the false view that older persons cannot respond to treatment because their mental and emotional problems are a result of physical deterioration and beyond the scope of psychotherapy. In reality, many mental and emotional disorders that affect older people can be treated and some can be reversed. More patients improve or recover than fail to respond to psychotherapy or other forms of help from mental health workers.

Myth of Asexuality. There is a commonly held belief that older persons lose their interest in sex, have no sexual needs and cannot function adequately as sexual partners. Although society generally strongly disapproves of any sexual activity for older persons and regards an interest in sexual activity after age 60 or 65 as abnormal, many older persons continue to have satisfactory and vital sexual experiences.

Myth of Family Dissolution. This myth is based on the belief that most families are not involved in the care of their older members and ship them off to institutions and nursing homes. In fact, only 5 percent of all elderly persons are found in an institution at any one time, and many live with or near their families.

Myth of Unproductivity. This myth is based on the belief that people withdraw from all active pursuits in old age and that they passively await the end of life. In fact, if given the opportunity, older people want to maintain their relationship with others and are interested in the world around them.

The Aging Process

Contrary to popular opinion, aging is not a disease; it is a natural process that involves significant organic, psychological and social changes. Most people can adapt to changes that come in later years, but many do not. How individuals react to change depends in large measure on what personal and social resources are available to them when they experience a significant loss. A great deal of strength is required to survive in old age, and survival depends on making a satisfactory adjustment to change and loss.

Many significant losses that persons experience come in late life when they have less psychic and physical energy to deal with them and have more difficulty maintaining their emotional balance. To help older persons cope with emotional problems, mental health workers need an understanding of the major physical, psychological and social changes that are part of the aging process. It is also important to be aware that these changes are interrelated. Physical and biological changes can affect mental and emotional functioning. Psychological processes—thinking and feeling—can affect physical functioning. Environmental factors such as changes in living arrangements can have a significant effect on mental functioning and emotional well-being.

Finally, efforts to help older persons cope with emotional problems must be based on a careful evaluation of each individual's unique history and present life situation and their capacity to adapt to change and to cope with the emotional problems that accompany loss. In short, a successful outcome of the helping process depends upon an understanding of what aging involves and how individuals attempt to deal with various sources of stress that result in emotional disturbances.

Physiological Changes

Contrary to popular opinion, aging is not a disease; it is a process involving certain physiological changes that result in a gradual slowing down in functioning. These changes vary from person to person. Some individuals have young bodies at age 70 and present only minor signs of aging. Others develop physiological dysfunctions before they reach age 65. However, there are some physiological changes that can be expected as people age. One of the most significant is a change in skeletal structure. Spines become shorter and shoulders begin to hump noticeably as a result of substantial loss of calcium that accompanies aging. Deterioration in cartilage creates difficulty in walking as joints become stiff and painful. The risk of serious bone fracture increases as the bones weaken. The problem is especially severe for older women who develop the most common bone disease, osteoporosis. However, the weakening of bone with aging can be slowed down by increasing the amount of calcium in the diet or using calcium tablets to supplement the diet. Estrogen therapy restores female hormones and helps the body maintain a better level of calcium. Physical exercise is also effective in preventing osteoporosis if practiced in the right amount on a regular basis.

As people age, the strength and size of their muscles decrease, causing them to appear weak and frail. Older persons have difficulty performing tasks that they could easily carry out when they were young. To those who take pride in their strength and vigor, this difficulty becomes a matter of much concern. Fortunately, older persons can maintain a satisfactory level of muscular strength and physical vigor if they follow an exercise program such as swimming or walking.

Other physiological changes involve vital organs, particularly the heart and lungs. Aging may cause the heart to grow weaker and cardiovascular problems may develop if the individual's arteries have hardened. Lungs sometimes become frayed, resulting in breathing difficulties, emphysema and chronic bronchitis. Most older persons will experience some discomfort because of heart and lung deterioration, but the vast majority are not seriously incapacitated and can carry on normal activities without difficulty. Moderate and sensible exercise helps strengthen heart muscles and increases the efficiency of the heart, lungs and blood vessels and may prolong life.

As individuals age, their capacity to fight off infectious diseases decreases due to a deterioration of the thymus gland that plays an important role in the functioning of the immune system. If the immune system fails, elderly persons are more likely to die from pneumonia—six or seven times as often as young adults who contract the disease. Changes in the immune system also account for a high incidence of cancer and tuberculosis in the aged population.

The neurological system also undergoes change as individuals age. These neurological changes result in a slowing down of the speed with which messages are transmitted from the brain to the nervous system. Older persons cannot respond as quickly to a given stimulus as can younger persons. Some motor functions, such as maintaining balance and coordinating body movements, are impaired. Sensory functions of vision, hearing and taste also diminish with the passage of time. The skin becomes less sensitive and results in some lack of awareness of cold or pain.

Despite some change in physiological functioning, many older persons still live normal, healthy lives. An increasing number not only enjoy good health, but are making valuable contributions to their families and to the communities in which they live. Advances in the relatively young science of gerontology hold even more promise for the future, but as Ruth Weg (1976) points out, "No one theory, intervention or incantation has proven to be the 'magic bullet' to slow or eradicate aging. The reasonable direction would seem to be to continue disciplinary and multidisciplinary research to work toward a maintenance and promotion or optimum functioning that is possible into the later years" (p. 277).

Psychological Changes

It is often assumed that individuals reach a peak in intelligence as young adults and that thereafter the ability to think deteriorates. Research has shown that there is no strong evidence to support that a decline in intelligence is an inevitable by-product of aging. There is evidence that older persons are not able to perform mental tasks as quickly as younger persons, but given problems in which speed is not of primary importance, older persons are able to function as adequately, though more slowly, as younger persons. This difference in speed does not indicate a deterioration in thinking capacity; it simply means that older persons are at a disadvantage in competing with younger persons. As Schaie points out, the everyday life of older persons does not require speed: "If an individual at age 30 is able to produce 40 words in three minutes but at age 70 can only produce 36 words, it is doubtful whether this decrement is going to make a lot of difference in his or her life. All it means is that it takes a little longer to come up with the right answers" (In Woodruff, p. 146).

In assessing the scores of older persons on intelligence tests, it is important to consider factors that affect the outcome of testing. It has been pointed out that when older persons approach the test, they become overanxious and that their fear of failing contributes to the lower performance. Therefore, the testing may not be an accurate measure of their intellectual ability. If they are put at ease and given adequate time to respond, their performance shows significant improvement. Moreover, many of the laboratory tests involve tasks that are meaningless and trivial for older persons. Therefore, they do not exert themselves in responding to what they regard as silly and unimportant questions. If they are asked to respond to questions that are relevant to their life situation, they are able to give thoughtful and intelligent answers.

Good health is also an important factor in intellectual functioning. Older persons who are in good health are also mentally alert. Those who have undergone a serious health crisis show some impairment in memory or thinking capacity. Exposure to a debilitating chronic disease also has an adverse effect on mental performance. Obviously, persons who suffer organic brain disease or injury are not able to concentrate or think clearly, but except for such cases, most older persons are able to carry on an active intellectual life.

Studies indicate that individuals who have been surrounded by an environment that encourages intellectual growth are at a considerable advantage in old age. Individuals who have been exposed to a wide range of reading materials, who have had an opportunity to travel and who have had a variety of social contacts are likely to maintain a high degree of intellectual ability and curiosity. Studies indicate that older persons who enroll in college often perform as well or better than their younger counterparts. Even at an advanced age, it is possible to develop new skills and master complicated tasks. Given good health and freedom from major impairments such as cerebral vascular disease and senile dementia, most individuals can expect to maintain a high level of mental competence beyond age 65 and even into their eighties.

One of the most common concerns of older persons is a loss of memory. As people pass from their fifties into their seventies, their ability to remember does diminish. Difficulty in recalling information or remembering past events is one of the most visible indications that the aging process has had an adverse effect on mental functioning. Older persons also have problems in assimilating new information and retaining it for recall. New information is more difficult to recall because it has not been stored well enough and is not as deeply processed as older information. If older persons are trained in the techniques of recall, some of these problems can be surmounted and their memory can be significantly improved. Neurologists are exploring the possibility of reversing memory loss in older persons by administering pharmaceuticals that change the chemistry of the brain. Some research indicates that a lack of choline acetyltransferase may be responsible for a loss of memory. Further research and experimentation may lead to discovery of additional methods that will help older persons who manifest serious memory disabilities.

Personality Changes

There is a widely held opinion that as people age they become rigid in their beliefs, attitudes and behavior; that they are set in their ways and resist change. They are also believed to be closed-minded and cannot accept new ideas or life-styles. Some older persons do match this description. They may persist in using inappropriate solutions and cling to beliefs that seem outmoded to others. However, rigidity is not a by-product of aging itself. It is a personality trait that individuals carry over from an earlier point in their lives. People who are rigid in old age have usually been inflexible in their forties and early fifties and stubbornly hold on to attitudes and values that became firmly entrenched when they were middle-aged. On the other hand, persons who have always been open-minded and mentally alert do not become inflexible as they age.

There is evidence that as they grow older, people do tend to become more cautious and are less likely to take risks. Being cautious serves as a protective mechanism that older persons use to avoid making mistakes in judgment because they undergo a decrease in self-confidence. Older persons are often viewed as incapable of making sound decisions in a society that places a premium on youthfulness. This places a special burden on older individuals to prove that they will not make mistakes in judgment, particularly if the matter at hand involves some major change in their life situation. Therefore, they avoid failure by not taking any risks if they cannot be certain of the outcome of making a decision or following a certain course of action.

It has been assumed that people become less active and withdraw from social contacts as they grow older. According to this view, the process of "disengagement" is a natural, almost inevitable and intrinsic part of aging. Included in this notion of disengagement is the belief that older people are really fulfilling a psychological need to become less involved with people and events in the outside world. Therefore, disengaged persons are happy in old age. This theory about the aging process has been challenged and modified because it has not been validated by other studies. These later investigations suggest that while some personality types are quite well satisfied by becoming disengaged, some older persons prefer to remain actively involved in a variety of activities and forms of personal interaction. Two groups that do want to withdraw are (1) those persons who are self-directed and are interested in the world but not in other people and (2) those who are ambitious and achievement oriented. Older persons who fall into these two categories view old age as a threat to their egos and protect themselves from an assault on their self-esteem by shutting themselves off from contacts with other people. A third group of older persons who are satisfied with disengagement are those who are either basically dependent or who are apathetic toward life. A minimum contact with others and a low level of activity seems to be the most satisfactory adjustment for such individuals in later adult life.

Do older persons voluntarily withdraw from an active life or does society force them into a state of disengagement? Should older persons simply be resigned to society's view that older persons should "take it easy" and enjoy a life of leisure? Or should they pursue an active life to prove that they are productive and useful? For some older persons, none of these choices is acceptable. Most older persons desire to stay active in order to maintain a sense of self-worth and at the same time desire to withdraw from some social commitments and pursue a less active life. No one solution is best for all elderly persons. But for those who do not choose to withdraw, society needs to provide opportunities for an active and full life in old age.

Sex and Aging

The sexual life of older persons has been shrouded in myths and misunderstanding. Society assumes that older persons are not interested in sex or that, if they are, they are not capable of carrying on an active sex life. However, studies have shown that many older persons do not lose their sexual desires and that they can continue to be sexually active into their eighties and beyond. Indeed, aging itself is not the chief factor in determining whether sex continues to be an important part of life as people grow older. More important are the negative attitudes and expectations about sexuality in old age that inhibit the continued enjoyment of sex after 60. Sex therapists have learned that if older persons are freed of mistaken views about sexual decline and are assured that they can have a satisfying sex life, most will remain active and gain a new sense of vigor and well-being.

Researchers have found that there are some significant physiological changes that affect the sexual functioning of men and women in later life. Men undergo hormonal changes. After age 50, there is a gradual decline in the testosterone level, but there is debate as to whether lower testosterone interferes with sexual functioning. However, most men do experience a decline in sexual responsiveness after age 50. It takes longer to achieve an erection, but once he has been sexually aroused, the male can maintain his erection for longer periods of time before he feels the urge to ejaculate. This comes closer to matching the needs of most females because they need more time to become aroused and experience orgasm. The ejaculation is usually not as intense and older men require more time to achieve a second erection after ejaculating.

As the female passes into her fifties, there is a general decline in her sexual responsiveness, in part due to the diminished production of estrogen and progesterone by the ovaries after menopause. The most important changes in the female occur about five years after she has ceased menstruating. The vagina walls become thinner and vaginal lubrication is reduced. However, the response of the clitoris to stimulation remains intact with increasing age. Because the clitoris plays a dominant role in sexual satisfaction for women, they can continue to reach orgasm despite some change in physiology. When the two sexes are compared, the female suffers less functional loss because her clitoris remains responsive to stimulation throughout her life, and she can continue to derive pleasure in sexual intercourse or through masturbation.

As people age, they lose their youthful body image. Because women are especially sensitive to their appearance, these changes may affect their attitudes about sex and lower their interest in sexual activity. Their capacity to engage in sex relations is not actually reduced, but their feeling that they are not sexually attractive may blunt their sex drive. Unfortunately, a negative body image can have a negative impact on sexual behavior, and a woman's perception of herself as an undesirable sex partner may interfere with her participation in sexual intercourse even though she retains her capacity to enjoy a healthy sex life.

How sexually active are older persons? There is a wide variation in this regard. Some individuals continue an active sex life beyond age 65, while others may be completely inactive at that age. People who have been sexually active earlier in life tend to remain active in later life. Studies indicate that those men who maintain a good level of sex in later life have a history of regular sexual experience and continue to express a strong interest in sex. Women who have consistently enjoyed sex throughout their lives engage in intercourse more frequently than women who have not enjoyed sex before they reached age 65.

The belief that sexual activity declines rapidly with age is challenged by Starr and Weiner in a study of a large number of older persons. They report that the average frequency of sexual activity according to age groups is as follows: (1) for persons age 60 to 69, the average is 1.5 times per week; (2) for persons age 70 to 79, the average if 1.4 times per week; (3) for those over 80, the average is 1.2 times per week. A Consumer's Union Report of 1984 covering 4,246 respondents shows that 81 percent of the women were active between age 60 and 70; 65 percent were active at age 70 and over. Men between age 60 to age 70 were sexually active in 91 percent of the cases, and 79 percent were active at age 70 or older. The substantially lower level of activity among women reflects the fact that many do not have access to a sexual partner after age 70. While only 50 percent of unmarried women were sexually active at age 70, 81 percent of married women reported that they were sexually active.

The Consumer Report survey found that 49 percent of women over age 50 experience orgasm every time or almost every time. Men reported a sharper decline in reaching orgasm. At age 50, 92 percent reached orgasm almost every time. At age 70 and over, the percentage fell to 70 percent. The survey also found that sexual enjoyment and satisfaction is not drastically reduced at age 60. Of the 800 persons who responded, 75 percent said that sex was the same or better than when they were younger. The report concludes: "Far from giving up their sexual selves, those older adults have achieved higher levels of sexual fulfillment. Their comments give power to the belief that the human mind is the most potent sex organ. Sex is better for these respondents because of greater understanding, increased self-awareness and greater appreciation of the sexual experience—all states of mind that can enhance and even transcend biology" (p. 44).

Adjusting to Retirement

No two individuals adjust to retirement in exactly the same way. For some, retirement brings a well-deserved release from pressure and responsibility. Those who are troubled by poor health are happy to be relieved from the physical strain of working. Some welcome retirement because it affords an opportunity to explore new interests and activities. Finally, there are those who find the inactivity forced on them by retirement is meaningless and intolerable.

How people will adjust to retirement will depend in part on the type of life-style they adopted before they left the work force. Such differences in life-style not only influence attitudes toward retirement but significantly affect the ability of retirees to make a successful transition to a nonworking role in later life. Lowenthal has identified five fairly well-defined life-styles: (1) obsessively instrumental life-style; (2) instrumental/other-directed life-style; (3) receptive/nurturant life-style; (4) autonomous life-style; (5) self-protective life-style. These different life-styles represent the value system of the people within that group, their relationship to other persons and the goals that determine their behavior.

Individuals who adopt an obsessive life-style are overachievers and work to the exclusion of all else, often to the point of exhaustion. The self-made businessman is the most conspicuous example. They are articulate about their aspirations, exaggerate their achievements and minimize their failures. They are extremely goal-oriented and once they achieve one goal, they must replace it by another in order to remain driven. Obsessive instrumental persons do not have much capacity for genuine empathy and seldom form strong ties of intimacy with others. These individuals seldom plan to retire, and it comes as a traumatic event for which they are ill-prepared. Consequently, they have great difficulty making a satisfactory adjustment to the role of a non-worker. They attempt to find a substitute for work but often find it is either impossible or appears to be impossible. If they cannot find a channel for pursuing their lifelong goals, they become depressed or even suicidal. Some develop a physical illness or neurotic symptoms.

Individuals who adopt an instrumental other-directed life-style also have a need to achieve, but they also want to devote some time and energy to their families as well. This is the masculine style that is prescribed for men in American society. To meet this standard, men must work hard, but they are also expected to be concerned about other qualities in life and to pursue work as a means of gaining peer acknowledgment, comfort and success. Individuals in this life-style are aware that there is a conflict in their goal to achieve and the need to form close intimate ties to others. When they retire, instrumental other-directed individuals undergo a period of temporary low morale but are usually able to find a goal other than work. They are more flexible than the obsessive-instrumental individuals and can re-orient their value system in order to make a fairly satisfactory adjustment to retirement.

A receptive-nurturant life-style is the one prescribed for women by American culture, although the feminist movement has redefined the role of women. Men may adopt this life-style in occupations such as teaching, child care, or social work. Some men may move from a non-obsessive life-style to a more nurturing style as they grow older. Persons in this group place a high value on intimacy and reciprocity. They are aware of the needs and goals of others. If receptive-nurturant people have worked in occupations that provided opportunities for close interaction with others, they may undergo a period of low morale when they retire unless they find other ways to gratify their need to play a nurturing role. Those who have a satisfying relation to their marital partner have less difficulty in retirement than those who cannot find a substitute form of gratification in their marriage. Most nurturant persons are unlikely to become depressed or suicidal because they are ingenious in forming new relationships after retiring. Some men may adopt a nurturant life-style after they retire because they are released from the pressure of instrumental performance and the demands for high achievement.

Reisman, Maslow and others have identified a group of persons who have a very complex life-style. They are autonomous persons who are capable of deep interpersonal relations, are creative and concerned with spiritual and moral values. Autonomous persons usually have a sense of mission and are strongly motivated to pursue a cause to which they are committed. Many who adopt this life-style are self-employed in such fields as art and writing that permit them to continue their endeavors in later life without interruption. For them, retirement does not pose any serious problems, because they can remain active and pursue their goals into their seventies and even into their eighties.

Some people adopt a self-protective life-style that is highly conventional. They are satisfied with having stayed out of trouble, avoiding conflict and surviving illness. Their goals and aspirations are very limited, and their relationship to others is shallow. Self-protective persons profess to be proud of their independence in old age. By this, they mean that they are free from demands that others might make on them. When they retire, work is replaced by a routine of self-protective activities and taking care of everyday survival needs. Contacts with others are not highly valued, and retirement may come as a relief from sustained interaction with others, especially if they are not forced to change their habitual pattern of living. If they become dependent because of poor health and need to rely on others for their care, self-protective individuals become very anxious and may develop paranoid projections as a reaction to having close contact with other people.

Loss of Status

The loss of status that comes with retirement is often deeply unsettling, especially for those who are ambitious and whose life has been built around their professional careers. Deprived of their former sources of gratification, they feel that they are useless. For them, retirement is a low blow to their self-esteem. Many have achieved prominent positions and been admired for their leadership. As retired persons, they miss the power and respect they once held and which is no longer accorded them. One executive who retired describes his reaction to this loss of status.

"After feeling important, valued, active, I now no longer felt needed and wanted. I felt the many years I had spent in building the organization were unappreciated. I even began to wonder if my professional reputation had been washed away by the mere act of retirement. I felt extremely sorry for myself."

Although most individuals' incomes will be reduced after they retire, the financial problem may not be their primary concern. In a study of 500 persons over age 60, Kutner (1956) and associates found that loss of status was a matter of concern for older persons. The study showed that income at retirement as compared to present income was not the chief factor in determining the individual's attitude toward retirement. "Since retirement forces many persons out of a lifelong routine into unwanted leisure, it is understandable that resistance to retirement should be so great," they conclude. "Further, it appears that it is not lack of money but a lack of a significant role that is one of the main sources of deprivation in retirement. The blow to the ego signified by retirement in our society is due to the fact that retirement tends to imply uselessness which is reinforced by the behavior of others toward retirees" (p. 89).

After they have retired, many individuals find that the goals they formerly pursued are no longer viable. A state of goalessness may follow and have devastating effects. Speaking from his own experience, a 65-year-old man, recently retired, recounts his feelings:

> I didn't realize that I faced a sudden, abrupt reversal in my life from long-range goals to short-range goals, and that hidden in this reversal was the terrible danger of goalessness with its consequent apathy, boredom and depression.... An individual can become hooked on goalessness as readily as on alcohol or drugs. Alcohol and drugs often follow goalessness because they provide a temporary way of blocking out self-dislike. (Bradford, p. 33)

Some retirees cling to the past in an effort to maintain their identity and sense of worth, but those who are flexible realize that old goals have to be replaced by new ones that relate to the present rather than the past. They begin to become involved in the needs of the communities in which they live and shift their attention to their families and friends. Some psychologists suggest that retirement can usher in a period of "growth expansion" that revitalizes older persons and gives new direction to their lives. Robert Peck (1968) points out that the changes involved in retirement often cause retirees to take a new look at themselves. Peck writes:

The chief issues might be put this way, "Am I a wonderful person only insofar as I can do a full-time job; or can I be worthwhile in other different ways—as a performer of several other roles, and also because of the kind of person I am?" For most men, the ability to find a sense of self-worth in activities beyond the job seems to make the difference between a despairing loss of meaning in life and a continued, vital interest in living. One critical requisite for successful adaptation to old age may be the establishment of a varied set of valued activities and valued self-attributes, so that any one of several alternatives can be pursued with a sense of satisfaction and worthwhileness. (P. 90.)

It is important to note that retirement does not adversely affect the majority of people. A study conducted at Cornell University indicated that most of the persons included in the survey reported that they were satisfied with their lives after retirement and that they did not undergo serious mental or emotional problems when they left employment. The authors of the study concluded that retirement did not seriously affect the mental health of the people surveyed. On the contrary, the study suggests that although a role loss may occur as people age, most older persons can adapt and maintain a positive view of themselves and with life as a whole (Strieb, 1971).

Adaptation to Aging

Old age is an important phase of the life cycle during which individuals make significant adaptations to change. During adolescence and early adult years, most individuals have the capacity to make transition from one stage to the next, but as people age, their ability to adapt to change is diminished, and the task becomes more difficult than in earlier years.

How well individuals adapt to aging depends in part on their ability to cope with transitions in their younger years. As Erikson points out, each phase in the life cycle requires a resolution of certain problems. Individuals who have successfully resolved these problems in the past can move on to the next stage in their development. For example, older individuals who have developed a trusting relationship to others in early life will accordingly be inclined to maintain a relationship of trust with others in old age. Those who have developed a sense of autonomy and self-identity during adolescence will be able to function with a high level of self-sufficiency and independence in later years. Individuals who have a history of satisfactory, intimate relationships with their marital partners and children will continue to have a fulfilling relationship to valued people in old age.

There is also some evidence to indicate that those who have gone through emotional disturbances earlier in their lives will be prone to experience emotional problems in the later years. For the most part, those who have a history of good mental health and emotional stability during their earlier years will be less likely to develop emotional problems in old age.

Moreover, those individuals who have been fortunate enough to have a good heritage, are in good health and have had a lifelong, stable relationship with family members are better equipped to adjust to aging than those who were not so well blessed. Good health, intelligence, adequate food and shelter and a good education certainly contribute to a happy and productive life; extreme poverty, broken families, poor education and a lack of medical care make adjustment to aging more difficult. In short, factors that contribute to a successful adaptation during adolescence, early adult life and the middle years also contribute to making a good adaptation to aging.

Social and Economic Problems

As people age, they often face problems of survival in a society that fails to provide adequate financial assistance, decent housing and a safe environment free from crime and violence. Not all older persons spend their "golden years" living in a social environment that is conducive to a happy and self-fulfilling existence.

Income and Poverty. Although the passage of the Social Security Act was passed to guarantee older persons would have adequate income when they were no longer able to work, poverty is still a major problem for the elderly. Indeed, the aged constitute the fastest growing poverty group in America. Even those who once had a decent standard of living can be thrown into poverty for the first time in old age. Moreover, the elderly are particularly hard hit by inflation. They live on fixed incomes and although Social Security payments have recently been adjusted for a rise in the cost of living, they do not absorb the loss due to inflation.

Housing and Living Arrangements. As people age, they are often uprooted from familiar surroundings and undergo drastic changes in their living arrangements. If they are unable to take care of their daily needs because of physical or mental impairment, older persons must find other living accommodations. There is a dearth of suitable board and room care for the aged. Facilities that are of high quality are beyond the means of most elderly people. Entering a nursing home or other long-term care facility can be a wrenching experience for older persons and their families. Fears of becoming dependent on others and losing control of one's life creates a high level of anxiety when an aged person must leave a family or environment and surrender much of his or her independence.

Many older persons live alone. About three-fourths of older men live in families that include the wife, but only one-third of older women live in families that include their husbands. More than three times as many older women live alone as do older men. Living alone contributes to feelings of loneliness that are associated with depression. Unless there is a supporting network of friends and relatives to whom older persons can turn, they may develop emotional problems.

Changing family living patterns have also made it difficult for adult children to share their homes with their aging parents. The extended family is still a source of support for many older persons, but a rapid trend toward smaller houses and increased mobility leaves some elderly parents without this source of help. Adult children, for the most part, still maintain an interest in their parents' welfare, but they are not always able to take them into their homes. Making a transition from independent living to other living accommodations therefore has become a major problem for many aged men and women.

Unfortunately, poverty sometimes forces older people into a state of homelessness. When rents soar in the inner city where many elderly persons live, the aged are often the victims of gentrification. They are evicted from the single-occupant hotels and must try to find another place to live on their meager incomes. For many, this is the first step on the road to homelessness—or as the National Coalition for the Homeless says—"a forced march to nowhere." Temporary shelter can provide overnight shelter and a hot meal, but many older homeless people spend their days walking about aimlessly, sleeping in bus terminals or seeking shelter in abandoned buildings.

Ageism. In our industrialized society that accords little respect or opportunity for self-determination, older persons may incorporate faulty perceptions about aging and come to embody the negative images that society portrays, as Louis Lowy (1979) points out:

> Many of us are suffering from a belief in stereotype about old age and the aged; and more aged people, in turn, are the victims of these stereotypes. This perhaps has become one of the major problems of old age; there is a social-psychological dictum which tells us that people behave according to the way in which they are expected to behave (P. 61).

The stereotypes of aging have created a set of attitudes that are highly prejudicial to older persons. Robert Butler (1975) has coined the term **ageism** which can be described as "a process of systematic stereotyping and discrimination against people because they are old, just as racism and sexism accomplish this with skin color and gender" (p. 12).

Groups have been formed all over the country to counteract ageism. Among them is the Gray Panthers formed by Maggie Kuhn. Founded in 1979, the Gray Panthers are engaged in a nationwide education program to challenge society's bias against older people, pointing out that the 22 million Americans who are 65 or older constitute a valuable resource that can make valuable contributions to both young and old. As Clark Tibbitts (1959) points out: "There are positive roles for aging people, through which they can make valuable contributions to society. This point of view calls for a new concept of aging—a concept that gives recognition to the positive as well as the negative aspects of maturation" (p. 127).

Summary

Aging involves significant biological, psychological and emotional changes with which older men and women must cope. Some experience little difficulty dealing with these changes, but others need help in surmounting the emotional difficulties that are part of aging. Mental health workers have an important role in this endeavor to enhance the quality of living for older Americans. Coping with the various demands of aging should not be the only concern that demands attention, as Lowy (1979) points out:

> When psychological, safety and esteem needs have been reasonably well met, people are ready to find gratification in self-actualization and understanding the world and their own existence in it; to take part in enjoying the gifts of life and nature; to enhance the quality of living for themselves and for their family, peers and friends, to engage responsibly and creatively to improve the lives of others (P. 43).

The achievement of this goal is the business of all helping professional persons. In the chapters that follow, various approaches to making life more meaningful for American senior citizens will be explored and the techniques employed to help older persons cope with emotional problems will be described.

Chapter 2

MENTAL AND EMOTIONAL DISORDERS

The vast majority of older persons remain mentally alert and emotionally healthy after they reach their sixty-fifth birthday. Unfortunately, some develop brain diseases or neurological disorders that impair their functioning, while others suffer from anxiety reaction, depression and other emotional disturbances. Still others react to aging by converting their psychological problems into physical complaints for which there is no organic basis. Problems of alcoholism and drug abuse, assumed to be found only among young persons, are also problems for the elderly as are difficulties in sexual functioning.

Brain Disease and Neurological Disorders

Two different forms of brain disease seriously impair the functioning of older persons: acute brain syndrome (delirium) and chronic brain disease (dementia).

Delirium is caused by a temporary malfunctioning of significant brain cells due to malnutrition, infection, inappropriate medication or some organic disease. Delirium causes the individual to become confused and disoriented. Patients suffering from delirium also have difficulty focusing their attention and remembering. In some cases, the patient becomes hyperactive, suffers from sleeplessness and may have hallucinations. Rarely is there a single cause of delirium. Therefore, treatment is based on a careful study of the psychological, chemical and behavioral aspects of the individual to determine the root of the dysfunctioning. Once the underlying cause of the disease is discovered, most of the mental impairment can usually be eliminated through appropriate treatment. Fortunately, the disorder can be reversed in about 20 percent of delirium patients.

Dementia (chronic brain disease) is usually unresponsive to treatment. This disease takes the form of impaired thinking, poor judgment and an inability to recognize objects and carry out a variety of motor activities.

In many cases, the individual undergoes marked changes in personality. The most devastating form of dementia is Alzheimer's disease, a major cause of death among the elderly. The disorder results from a shrinkage of the brain, the destruction of brain cells and serious damage to the connections between them. As the person ages, the brain continues to deteriorate and there is no treatment that can arrest the progress of the disease. As yet, the cause of Alzheimer's disease is not known, but research indicates that chemical abnormalities, especially large amounts of aluminum, are present. The immune system also seems to be impaired. Genetic factors may also be involved, although it is uncertain why some families are predisposed to contract the disease.

Although not typically present in cases of Alzheimer's-type dementia, arteriosclerosis and atherosclerosis is a cause of dementia in about 10 to 20 percent of all cases. Many older persons who manifest symptoms of dementia also suffer from heart disease or diabetes. If the arteries are in poor condition, brain cells are damaged because of insufficient blood being supplied to the brain. Because the arteries are blocked, more brain cells are destroyed as the person ages. Although a few persons can undergo some brain damage and yet live out their lives without further problems, most deteriorate over months or years. Proper medication may ameliorate some symptoms of dementia or slow the progress of the disease temporarily, but there is as yet no cure for dementia.

One of the most common neurological disorders of old age is Parkinson's disease. During the course of the illness, certain brain cells fail to function, causing the patient to develop a rigid posture as the muscles become stiff and immobile. As the disease progresses, other symptoms appear. Facial expression is severely strained, the patient becomes agitated, aggressive or irritable. Many Parkinson's disease patients also become seriously depressed. The emotional problems are often as severe as the physical deterioration that accompanies the illness. Parkinson's disease is caused by a failure in the functioning of a small center deep inside the brain to send messages to surrounding brain cells. Although the nervous disorder cannot be cured, medication does help patients function more easily. The missing chemical in the brain, dopamine, can be replaced by a similar substance, L-dopa. Patients also show improvement if they engage in regular exercise to keep their muscles from becoming immobile.

Stroke is a neurological disorder that afflicts more than a quarter million people in the United States, and 75 percent of them are over age 65. Along with cancer and heart disease, strokes rank high as the cause of death among the elderly. About one-half of those who suffer a stroke do survive, but of these survivors, one-half are seriously disabled. In any stroke, a core of brain tissue is irreparably damaged. Multiple strokes usually result in some degree of disorientation and/or memory loss. The lower portion of the face opposite the brain damage is often weakened or paralyzed. The paralysis following a stroke affects both the upper and lower extremities, but the upper are usually more often impaired.

In addition to the physical impairment, stroke victims face severe emotional problems. They cannot rely on their minds or bodies, and much of their past is irretrievably lost as their memory fails. These important losses and changes in mental and physical functioning may result in a profound grief reaction. Many become depressed, angry, bitter, anxious or hopeless. However, a rigorous program of rehabilitation will help patients cope with the emotional trauma and enable them to regain an amazing degree of normal functioning.

Depression

Depression is by far the most prominent emotional disorder among older persons. Depression takes on several forms and may go unrecognized unless an accurate assessment is made when symptoms first appear. These symptoms fall into five major categories: (1) dysphoria, including feelings of sadness, apathy and boredom; (2) behavioral deficits, such as withdrawal from social participation and decreased activity; (3) behavior excesses, including complaints about one's life situation, guilt feelings, doubts about one's abilities; (4) somatic symptoms such as headaches, sleep problems, poor appetite; and (5) cognitive manifestations including persistent feelings of low self-esteem, failure, self-blame and hopelessness.

Not all the above symptoms are found in any individual patient, and there is no universally accepted criteria to determine the number or severity of symptoms that constitute a depression. However, the following symptoms are set forth in the DSM–III manual as a basis for making a diagnosis of a depressive illness:

1. The essential feature of a depression is a dysphoric, depressive mood manifested by any of the following: sadness, hopelessness, "feeling low," discouraged, blue, empty and without feeling, weepiness, irritable and worried. Only sophisticated individuals are

likely to report feeling depressed. An absence of capacity for pleasure manifested by loss of interest in former activities is typically present. The mood is reported as different from that following the death of a loved one.
2. Poor appetite or weight loss of more than 1 pound per week when dieting, or increased appetite are also typical. The former is more characteristic of agitated depression and the latter of retarded type.
3. There is often an alternation of sleep pattern. Insomnia, especially with frequent awakening during the night or early morning not due solely with the urge to urinate, with difficulty returning to sleep, is present in agitated depression. Increased sleep, often manifested by difficulty in getting up in the morning, is typical of retarded depression.
4. There is a loss of the subjective sense of energy, or easy fatigability.
5. Objective psychomotor agitation or retardation are usually present.
6. There is objective or subjective difficulty with concentration or thinking, which may be manifested in inattention, apathy, indecisiveness, blocking. Patients will often report that they are unable to read a newspaper or book without losing their place, or notice that they are unable to remember what they have just read, yet they may worry or ruminate about matters and not be able to come to closure with what used to be insignificant daily problems.
7. There is verifiable loss of interest in previously pleasurable activities, including sexual drive.
8. Self-reproach or guilt of unrealistic proportion or in an obsessional manner is present.
9. The person has thoughts of suicide or death or the equivalent.

Severe Depression. Depressive illness may be mild, moderate or severe. Most mild depressions usually result from a significant loss or an undesired change in the life of the individual. Severe depressions seem to develop without such a precipitating event and appear to be associated with chemical and organic changes that produce depressive reactions. Characteristics that indicate a severe depression are:

1. Inability to function alone in carrying out normal tasks such as feeding and personal hygiene.
2. Difficulty in communication due to muteness or lack of comprehension.
3. Psychotic symptoms of a nihilistic or guilt-ridden nature may be

present. Characteristic delusions include the belief that the body is decaying or giving off offensive odors. There may be auditory hallucinations that involve voices making critical statements or accusations. Unrealistic feelings of guilt about past behavior are also present in some cases.

Manic-Depressive Illness. Manic-depressive illness (bipolar depression) is not as common among older persons as is unipolar depression. Individuals who are diagnosed as manic depressive manifest a history of depressive mood episodes that alternate with states of euphoria or irritability. In the manic phase, patients exhibit hyperactivity, increased talking and flights of ideas. There is also a marked decrease in the need for sleep and an increase in excessive behavior such as buying sprees, reckless driving, or hypersexuality. Some symptoms of manic-depressive illness may be present in patients who are suffering from other disorders including agitated depression, organic brain syndrome, drug-induced psychosis, hyperthyroidism, or catatonic excitement. A history of previous episodes of manic reactions is helpful in making a differential diagnosis. The presence of affective disorders in the patient's family is also a clue to the diagnosis of manic depression. Suicide is a major problem in both the manic and depressive phase of the illness, and clinicians should be particularly aware of this possibility.

Disguised (Masked) Depression. Some older persons who are going through a depressive illness resist admitting that they are experiencing unfamiliar feelings of sadness and do not seek out treatment for their distraught emotional state. Instead, they mask their emotional problems in the guise of physical complaints because they feel that admitting their true feelings would indicate a personal failure or a "mental breakdown." Usually, the patient presents a number of somatic complaints that do not respond to medication. Among the most frequent complaints are feelings of weakness, headaches, constipation and abdominal pains. Disguised depression can usually be identified because the individual begins to show signs of restlessness, irritability and anger at the onset of the disorder. Significant changes in behavior also indicate the possibility of a disguised depression. Individuals who are usually cooperative and friendly may become negativistic and argumentative. Although these changes are obvious to others, the depressed patient will refuse to recognize that there is an emotional problem troubling him. Masked depression is often a "missed depression" because the patient obscures the real nature of his illness from the physician as well as other persons who try to be of help. Differentiation between hypochondrical disorders and depression can present difficulties, and older persons who submit to a wide range of treatment for medical problems may develop a full-blown depression that goes untreated.

Medical Disease and Depression. Depressive symptoms are often found in patients who are suffering from chronic diseases such as cancer, arthritis and heart disease. In some cases, the medical disease may actually cause depression, in particular, Parkinson's disease, brain tumors, diseases of the thyroid or adrenal glands, diabetes, multiple sclerosis and serious kidney disease. Some drugs that are prescribed to treat these diseases bring about a depressive reaction. Among these drugs that produce depression as a side effect are: digitalis, reserpine, Inderal, Aldomet, steroids, cancer drugs and L-dopa. Depression that results from the use of these drugs will frequently diminish when the patient discontinues their use. Because multiple factors can produce identical clinical symptoms of depression, patients need to be evaluated by a physician who is familiar with the relationship between the brain and physical symptoms in older persons. In addition, psychological tests are useful in order to determine if the depressive symptoms are due to organic brain damage or other medical problems associated with emotional and mental disorders. The evaluation should also include a complete review of the patient's medical and psychiatric history. Family members and others who are well acquainted with the patient can supply information that is helpful in determining the nature of the illness, and a history of the patient's family is a valuable adjunct in the formulation of a complete diagnostic picture.

Treatment of Depression. Most depressions respond well to the use of antidepressant drugs such as Elavil, Norpramin, Sinequan, Trofranil, Aventyl and Vivactil. These antidepressants reverse chemical processes that produce depression, and two out of three patients respond well to the first use of this form of medication. Some side effects such as slight sedation, dry mouth, constipation and dizziness are reported, but most of these are not severe or long-lasting. If tricylic antidepressant medication fails to relieve the symptoms, monoamine oxidase inhibitors (MAO) such as Marplan, Nardil and Parnate are effective in treating depression, especially when the illness is associated with anxiety and phobias. Lithium carbonate is most effective in treating bipolar depression and is generally used on a continuing basis to prevent the recurrence of the disease. Most tranquilizers are used in cases of profound depression that are accompanied by hallucinations and delusions. Minor tranquilizers such as Valium are useful in short-term treatment to help anxious and agitated individuals feel more comfortable. In some cases, these tranquilizers are used to control symptoms in the early stages of the depression until the antidepressants have had time to become effective.

Electroconvulsive therapy is now regarded as a very safe treatment for depression. It is often the treatment of choice in patients who are delusional, who are severely withdrawn or who are highly agitated. When medication does not reduce the depression, ECT usually brings about dramatic results. Severely withdrawn patients become interested in their environment, begin to enjoy food and can communicate with others. Moreover, these results occur in days instead of weeks, and ECT has proven effective in nine out of ten patients. Temporary memory loss that occurs after ECT can be diminished by using unilateral treatment to the right hemisphere and by administering the treatment every other day. Older individuals respond well to ECT. Often, only four to six treatments enable the patient to function normally. Once the patient shows improvement, antidepressants are usually prescribed to prevent relapse.

Late Life Depression. A 67-year-old man reports to his physician that he is having difficulty sleeping, has lost weight and is fatigued most of the time. His wife advises the doctor that her husband is withdrawn, moody and irritable. She observed that his behavior changed within a year after he retired.

Mrs. C, age 68, is referred to a counselor by the doctor who is treating her 70-year-old husband for terminal cancer. She is worried about her husband's condition and feels that not enough is being done to cure his illness. Mrs. C has asked for sleeping pills to control her insomnia and also complains about pains in her abdomen.

Mrs. J, age 69, is a widow. Her married daughter has asked a counselor for advice regarding her mother's behavior. Mrs. J has continued grieving over the death of her husband for almost two years. At times, she talks as if he were still alive and present. She spends most of the day in her room. If friends visit, she is only interested in talking about her husband and her loneliness.

Each of these individuals is facing different circumstances, but they all show symptoms that are common in late life depression. In some cases, apathy and listlessness are predominant characteristics. In other cases, loss of memory and somatic complaints are symptomatic of depression. Since somatic complaints are often associated with aging, it is difficult to determine if they are secondary to depression or whether they represent a physiological dysfunction. If the individual shows signs of apathy, is listless or is expressing a sad demeanor, the somatic complaints may be reflecting an emotional problem even if the client denies that he or she "feels depressed."

Some depressed individuals also manifest behavior that gives the impression of cognitive dysfunctioning, especially impaired memory. However, when tested, these clients perform within normal limits, indicating that there is no organic brain disease or cognitive impairment. On the other hand, some individuals who are depressed also do have an organic brain defect and the depression may then be the first sign of brain disease. In all cases, it is important to determine if the depression is independent of any brain impairment.

Assessing a late life depression must take into account the effect of loss and stress as a cause of a serious emotional problem. Older persons are highly vulnerable to loss of a significant other person or spouse. There are few opportunities for them to form new relationships and their ability to respond is diminished. The accumulation of stress and a prolonged period of grieving can have a devastating effect on older persons. Depression after a loss is not an abnormal temporary reaction, but if the symptoms continue over a year, the individual is probably undergoing a serious mental health problem that requires active intervention.

Depression in older persons may often be related to their cognitive style. Depressed persons have a negative view of themselves and the world around them. These negative self-perceptions are likely to increase with age and create a mental state that results in chronic despondency. The stereotype of aged persons as unworthy and useless that is so widely accepted contributes to this negative self-image and feelings of depression. Cognitive therapy is useful in helping older persons become aware that their thoughts have a strong influence on their feelings of depression and teaches them to apply this awareness in everyday living.

Although it is assumed that younger-age patients respond to therapy better than older persons, there is no evidence to support this claim. One study of older depressed patients showed that those who were age 60 at the onset of depressive symptoms had a good recovery rate and were less likely to be readmitted to the hospital after a twenty-month follow-up than those who had an onset of depression earlier in life(Kay, Roth and

Hopkins, 1955). In fact, older persons have a relatively good prognosis and can be restored to normal functioning after being treated for depression. Clients who experience reoccurrence of depression respond well to treatment procedures that were effective in previous episodes. The use of lithium carbonate for treating manic-depressive psychosis is bringing excellent results. Antidepressants show a high degree of success in treating a variety of depressive illnesses. Psychological approaches used in conjunction with medication provide valuable help in restoring and maintaining good mental health.

Suicide

Suicide is a serious problem among older persons. In 1970, over 31 percent of all suicides were committed by persons over sixty-five years of age. The suicide rate is especially high for older white males, and there is a steady increase at each succeeding age level. Among men 65 to 69, the suicide rate is 37.4 per 100,000. The peak is reached at age 80 to 84 when the rate increases to 51.4 suicides per 100,000 (Pfeifer, 1977). Moreover, older persons are more likely to carry out suicide attempts successfully than younger men. Nearly half of elderly persons who attempt suicide complete the act, but only one out of eight younger persons carry the attempt to conclusion.

Persons who attempt suicide are seriously depressed before they commit suicide. The key factor that is present in high-risk cases is a sense of hopelessness and extreme pessimism. A serious physical problem is also a frequent precursor of suicide. Persons who are single and living alone, or older persons who have lost a significant other, are also prone to suicide. Serious financial problems are also associated with some cases of suicide. A combination of these factors (poor health, financial problems and lack of a supportive network) when the older individual is depressed indicates a high possibility that suicide will occur.

In assessing the potential of suicide, it is important to determine if the individual has made his intention known in one of the following ways: (1) a direct statement of intention; (2) a statement that he or she would be better off dead; (3) expressing a wish to die; or (4) discussion of various ways to commit suicide. Studies indicate that those who have a specific plan for taking their lives and who have designated a certain time when they will carry out the act are most likely to carry out a suicide attempt (Murphy and Robbins, 1968).

The approach to preventing suicide involves several aspects: (1) establishing a relation of trust with the older person; (2) helping the person arrange for medication to relieve the depression or any underlying illness that needs medical attention; (3) providing help in solving immediate problems that the person presents; and (4) enlisting the interest of persons who can provide a supportive network that is often absent.

Counseling that is directed to helping older persons make a satisfactory adjustment to the changes brought about in the normal process of aging is an important part of helping those who are rigid and inflexible in personality. A study of aged veterans suggests that men who manifested evidence of suicidal ideation or who had made attempts to end their lives were extremely rigid and had built their lives around ambition, hard work and perfection. They also had strong depressive feelings combined with anger and hostility toward others (Wolff, 1969). When they aged, their control over their aggressive impulses could not find expression against other people, and they then turned their hostility inward. These findings indicate that suicide may be described as one way that older people adapt to the aging process. Breed and Hufline (1979) argue that adaptability is the key factor in suicide. "Adaptability is a characteristic of individuals that enhances their ability to survive, socially and psychologically, as well as physically. Its opposite is rigidity and inflexibility, the inability to change roles and goals. The rigid individual will have difficulty dealing with transitions and situational change. Such a person becomes a higher suicide risk to the extent that other basic elements are present—such as isolation and failure in a role to which he or she is deeply committed" (p. 307).

Therapy is directed toward helping persons recognize that the feelings of hopelessness are a result of illogical thinking and erroneous assumptions. Alternatives to suicide may be openly discussed so that the depressed person can evaluate his present life situation in a realistic and rational way. Exploring how the individual wants to live out the rest of his life or what he wants yet to accomplish as unfinished business can often provide an alternative that the depressed individual may consider.

Hypochondriasis

Hypochondriasis is almost as common in older persons as is depression. One study indicated that 63 percent of depressed patients had hypochondrical symptoms and that these symptoms preceded the depression in one-third of the cases. In one-fourth of the cases, the dominant symptom was hypochondriasis and the presence of depression was apparent only after direct questioning of patients (Alarcon, 1964). The diagnosis of hypochondriasis is also complicated by the fact that many older persons have somatic complaints that are the normal results of the aging process. In most cases, such complaints are related to some organic cause, in contrast to hypochondriasis.

The complaints of hypochondrical patients cover a wide range of ailments, especially pains in muscles or bone and symptoms of discomfort in the digestive system. The patients are preoccupied with physical functions and are greatly concerned about their health when there is no indication of an organic problem. Reassurance and careful medical examination do not bring about a diminution of the patient's concerns, and they continue to reject any suggestion that their complaints have a psychological origin, even after thorough exhaustive tests show no evidence of a medical problem. Early and von Mering (1960) reported the history of a 70-year-old woman over a period of 18 years. During this time, she was seen by over 226 physicians and had extensive physical examinations, including 138 laboratory tests. At the end of this time, she insisted that doctors had not really made an effort to get at the cause of her complaints, and she continued to seek out additional treatment for them.

Some studies indicate that primary hypochondriasis can be distinguished from secondary hypochondriasis. Some individuals present somatic complaints and exhibit no symptoms of other disorders, while secondary hypochondriasis involves feelings of anxiety or depression in addition to concerns about health. Those who fall into the latter group are found to have made suicide attempts and have problems in sexual adjustment. Primary hypochondriasis seems to be a reaction to a stressful situation, analogous to a reactive depression, and in many cases the somatic complaints disappear within a relatively short period.

One of the earliest contributors to the study of hypochondriasis in older persons summarizes the psychodynamics of the illness. E. W. Busse (1954) indicates that patients use the somatic symptoms in the following ways:

1. To symbolize and make concrete one's sense of defectiveness and deterioration.

2. To serve as a ticket in interaction with caretakers, physicians and nurses.
3. To displace anxiety from other areas of concern.
4. To serve as an identification with a deceased loved one through displaying similar symptoms.
5. To serve as punishment and to relieve guilt.
6. To avoid or inhibit unwanted behavior or interaction.
7. To punish others.
8. To regulate or reduce interpersonal intimacy.

In general, this emotional illness may represent a reaction to a life change that involves loss of status and curtailment of activities that come with aging. The secondary gains that result from concern about their health brings about some gratification to individuals who have no other sources of gratification. The somatic complaints may also be a defense against feelings of guilt or failure. Being ill also excuses the patient from assuming responsibilities that he or she finds difficult and from which he can be relieved because of physical incapacity and health problems. Moreover, the attention that individuals gain from a repetition of their complaints reinforces their symptoms and they become a persistent way of coping with the aging process.

Reports of effective treatment of hypochondriasis are few. In some cases, the patient whose symptoms are secondary to a depression will respond to anti-depressant medication. If the patient is found to be deficient in social skills and has few sources of satisfaction, treatment is directed toward initiating positive interaction with others and improvement in appearance and behavior. During the time that patients are being taught to reshape skills in interaction, they agree not to seek out medical help for a limited time. Family members are instructed to change their response to the patient, to refrain from reinforcing the symptoms by giving attention to the individual's complaints.

Paranoid States

Paranoid states are disorders in which persecutory or grandiose delusions are the dominant characteristics. The delusions are likely to include reports of imaginary plots. These patients often appear to be mentally ill, but their intellectual functions, their abilities to think, are not impaired. In most cases, the delusions are very circumscribed and appear only under specific conditions or only under severe stress. Because these individuals have delusions that are disturbing to persons whom they contact, they are avoided or they are referred from one agency to another. Estimates of the prevalence of the disorder in older persons vary, but reports indicate that 16 percent of patients admitted to psychiatric hospitals developed paranoid symptoms before they reached age 60. The incidence of the disorder may be considerably higher, because older persons having paranoid symptoms do not usually present themselves from treatment and are wary about those who investigate their complaints.

Four types of paranoid states have been described by Allen and Claw (1950):

1. Consistent overaction to environmental annoyances.
2. Episodic paranoid conditions with a generally favorable prognosis.
3. Paranoid states that may be associated with involutionary psychosis and have a poor prognosis.
4. Paranoid states associated with organic brain disease where recovery is precluded.

Persons with brain disease represent a sizeable proportion of older persons presenting paranoid states. An organic brain disease was found to be present in 13 of 61 patients with late life paranoid states (Post, 1966). Some patients appear to have been borderline schizophrenics, but late life paranoid states are usually distinct from paranoid schizophrenia.

Medication has been shown to be effective in the treatment of paranoid states. Phenothiazine has been reported to have brought remission in 43 or 71 patients, and these gains were sustained between one and three years. In addition, supportive psychotherapy is usually employed to alleviate symptoms. A reality approach that directly attacks the patient's delusions is not useful. Therapy that accepts the patient's symptoms as a result of a feeling of helplessness and vulnerability can sometimes help the patient surmount the fears that plague him or her.

Because paranoid ideation is often found to be associated with loss of hearing, aids that restore the impairment often bring about dramatic improvement. Older persons may sometimes complain that others are talking about them, but this is not an indication of a psychosis in every situation. The delusions can be rather easily corrected by providing a reliable hearing aid. Social isolation has also been identified as an important contributing factor in the development of paranoid states. The prior social adjustment of some such individuals is marginal. They are likely to live alone, have few close friends or relatives and have a history of difficulty in forming and maintaining personal interrelationships. Social isolation may be due to a recent loss or stressful event such as death or physical illness of friends or relatives. Treatment that helps these patients cope with loss and that motivates them to engage in interacting with others is indicated as an important adjunct to the use of medication to relieve the most disturbing symptoms.

Late life paranoid states do not seriously affect the individual's ability to take care of himself and most can continue to live in the community, especially if the patient undergoes treatment. Institutionalization will only worsen the patient's condition. Although complete remission may not be achieved, these older persons can benefit from therapy and many show good prospects for improvement if they are offered treatment in the early stages of the disorder.

Anxiety Reaction

Elderly persons tend to become anxious about a number of things: loss of a check, a new medical symptom or a financial problem. Most such anxiety reactions are temporary and present no serious difficulty in functioning. However, anxiety can become so pervasive that the individual is worried about all aspects of his life and environment. Vague feelings that some disaster is about to befall him and dread about some future event can produce a serious state of emotional disturbance that results in insomnia, heart palpatation, diarrhea, or butterflies in the stomach. When anxiety becomes this pervasive, patients become chronically miserable and their health begins to suffer. In some cases, anxiety becomes attached to some specific fear, but in other cases the patients attach their worries to a succession of concerns. Fear about a brain disease or a brain tumor are characteristically found among older persons who become overly anxious, and in some cases it is difficult to determine if the symptoms represent a depressive illness or an anxiety neurosis. Therefore, a careful evaluation is essential before a sound treatment approach can be put in place. A medical examination is useful in order to rule out the presence of certain medical illnesses that cause nervousness and anxiety in older persons.

Psychotherapy can be effective in reducing the patient's level of anxiety. Use of relaxation exercises are also useful in reducing stress and tension. Biofeedback is also a technique that can be used to help patients reduce their level of anxiety. Helping patients identify the situations that produce stress is an important aspect of counseling and psychotherapy. Once sources of anxiety have been identified, the patient can be helped to deal with them more effectively. As the patient becomes more confident in his or her ability to deal with life situations, the anxiety will diminish.

Medication is also useful in treating anxiety reactions. Mild tranquilizers (Valium, Librium, Serax) usually control symptoms but should not be used for more than a few weeks. Antidepressants such as Tofranil, Noparmin or Sinequan may also be effective medications.

Alcohol and Drug Abuse

Alcohol problems do occur in the elderly population. Reports indicate that 10 percent of older patients seen in clinics and hospitals are involved in alcohol abuse. Because alcoholism can mimic several other psychopathologies, it is important to investigate the possibility of alcoholism when symptoms of depression, schizophrenia or disorientation are present. Studies indicate that many elderly alcoholics began drinking late in life and are likely to have organic brain damage. They are persons who live alone, tend to be socially isolated and are likely to present medical problems in addition to alcohol abuse. Fortunately, alcoholism can be treated more successfully in older persons than in younger persons. In severe cases, a temporary period of hospitalization is indicated with outpatient follow-up care to help patients maintain sobriety. Organizations such as Alcoholics Anonymous are exceptionally effective in helping older, as well as younger, persons gain lasting control over their drinking problem.

Older persons are the largest consumers of legal medications. Although they make up about 10 percent of the total population, they receive 25 percent of all prescribed drugs, partially because they have a higher incidence of chronic illness. Elderly persons also tend to self-medicate and tend to use over-the-counter drugs to relieve pain and correct problems such as arthritis, constipation and insomnia. In general, older persons are likely to react adversely to medications, even in normal dosages, and experience more frequent side effects than younger persons.

Sleeping pills (hypnotics) are especially dangerous, because even normal dosage can produce confusion in older persons. Careless prescribing of drugs by physicians sometimes leads to the misuse of powerful drugs when the doctor does not recognize the nature of the patient's problems and symptoms. To ensure that drugs are not misused, the following rules are applied: (1) know the pharmacological action of the drug; (2) use the lowest possible dosage; (3) know the cause of symptoms before prescribing the drug; and (4) review the effect of the drug at regular and frequent intervals. Careful evaluation and follow-up is especially important in prescribing hypnotics and anti-anxiety medication.

Sexual Dysfunctions

For most older persons, a decline in physical energy brings on a diminution of sexual activity. Kinsey and associates found that 30 percent of men age 70 were not sexually active. Among these 70-year-old men, 27 percent were impotent. At age 75, more than half were unable to achieve an erection.

Several psychological factors account for sexual impotence in older men. Most older men become concerned about their sexual performance, and the anxiety that is generated by their fear that they may not be able to carry out the sexual act is a major factor in erectile incapacity. As men age, they cannot achieve an erection as quickly or easily as at an earlier age. Their ejaculations are not as copious or forceful as those of younger men. Yet, it is possible for older males to enjoy a satisfying sexual relation despite these differences if they are informed and psychologically prepared for some changes in sexual functioning.

Some problems in sexual functioning arise when the man believes he should not engage in sex because of health reasons. Men who have had a heart attack often fear that the exertion involved in sexual intercourse is life-threatening. Studies show that the heart rate is slower during orgasm than when an individual engages in everyday activities such as walking up a flight of stairs. Much of this undue anxiety can be traced to misinformation. Two-thirds of physicians who treat men for heart ailments do not give them any information about the effect their condition might have on their sexual functioning. Given accurate information, most older men who are myocardial patients will rest assured that they can resume a normal sex life without fear.

Depressive illness is often a cause of sexual impotence in older men, especially when antidepressant medication is prescribed to treat the illness. Blocking agents that are used to treat hypertension can reduce the flow of blood to the penis and have an inhibiting effect on the libido. An excessive use of alcohol may also be a factor in some cases.

Stress can also produce sexual impotence. Some older men worry about their health, their financial situation or problems in their families. Sadness and grief over a personal loss is especially devastating and produces immediate impotence. When the source of stress is gone, the sexual problem diminishes and sexual activity is resumed.

Orgasmic dysfunctioning in women is a common problem, particularly among older women who have a history of irregular or unsatisfactory coital experience earlier in their lives. The onset of menopause is a trying period for some women due to the body's inability to produce a sufficient amount of estrogen. However, this condition can be corrected by regular use of hormone supplements. The psychological effects of menopause can also cause a decline in sexual interest and activity if the woman regards the cessation of menstruation as a sign of aging and a loss of femininity. Changes in physical appearance are also a source of concern for women when they believe that they are losing their sexual attractiveness.

Women also react strongly to certain types of sexual surgery. Some women believe that the removal of the womb will cause them to develop masculine traits or that they will lose their sexual desire. Because there is no basis for these concerns, physicians need to assure their patients that a hysterectomy does not change women, that the surgery does not affect their ability to perform or decrease their desire for sex. Husbands also need to be assured that their wives can resume a normal sex life after surgery.

Mastectomy is usually an emotionally traumatic experience for women. Although there is no physiological reason for a decline of sexual desire or competence, women fear that they will lose their sexual attractiveness. Professional counseling can often help both husband and wife work through the emotional and psychological problems involved so that they can continue a satisfactory sexual relationship. Women who have had surgery can also turn to others who have undergone the operation and who have learned to overcome the emotional problems involved in dealing with the loss of an important part of their bodies.

Many, if not most, sexual problems in sexual relations involve a difficulty in the relationship between the sex partners. Therefore, sex therapy requires cooperation by both to bring about a resolution of sexual dysfunctioning. Sex therapy is based on the premise that a change in attitude and behavior and an improvement of the quality of the overall interaction between the partners is essential to a successful outcome. Several features are common to this approach in sex therapy. The steps include: providing information about sexual functioning; changing negative attitudes about sex; eliminating performance anxiety and increasing communication between partners. Behavioral steps are used to improve sexual techniques and bring about better sexual performance.

Giving older persons permission to engage in sex and providing knowledge about slower sexual responsiveness in later life can do much to alleviate anxiety about feelings of sexual inadequacy.

Stress and Aging

The later years are often characterized by a series of emotionally hazardous events: severe illness, retirement, frequent or abrupt changes in living arrangements, loss of a spouse and death of close friends and companions. It is not unusual for these stressful events to follow in rapid succession, increasing the likelihood of a severe emotional reaction as a result of accumulated stress. Unfortunately, many older persons have limited personal, financial and social resources available when they are forced to cope with stress and have difficulty adapting to new situations. Early recognition of stress can prevent the development of serious emotional problems if help is extended soon after the stressful event occurs.

The high incidence of depressive illness among the elderly can be traced to the many stressful events that occur in later life. Post (1962) found that losses or the threat of losses preceded the onset of depression in about two-thirds of elderly patients. As previously stated, most stressful events are related to loss: loss of family members, financial or social status, or loss of mental and physical functioning. Even if the loss is only perceived as real, such as memory loss, the stress is as profound as if it were real. Illness appears to be a prominent stressful event that precipitates depression in older persons (Kay, Roth, and Hopkins, 1955). Depression also seems to be associated with feelings of helplessness when older persons perceive themselves as having little control over their lives.

Environmental factors are also frequent sources of stress for older persons and must be taken into account in assessing mental, emotional and behavioral problems that are likely to be considered abnormal. For example, older persons may present severe anxiety symptoms or patterns of paranoid ideation that appear to be "abnormal." However, when taken in the context of the social environment, the anxiety and suspiciousness is found to be based in part on reality. Living in a crime-ridden area where assaults on older persons are a part of everyone's experience may well cause a reasonable concern about leaving the security of one's apartment and exposing oneself to the risk of becoming the victim of a mugger.

Lack of financial resources is often a problem for older persons who live on the limited amount of money provided by Social Security payments. Providing adequate support, decent housing and medical care is therefore a major concern for those who are charged with the responsibility of helping older persons cope with stress. In short, a social policy that is designed to significantly reduce or eliminate social and financial sources of stress is essential as a reasonable and effective approach to solving the emotional problems of aging.

Implications for Intervention

The view that depression and other emotional disorders among the elderly are related to stress indicates that mental health workers must be aware of the serious impact of stress-producing events in later life. Several implications are specially worthy of note.

First, the medical model of psychopathology has its uses but also has limitations in the treatment of disorders among elderly persons. It calls attention to the organic basis of pathology and the case of various forms of somatic therapy, such as medication that can be effective in controlling symptoms. However, the medical model places emphasis on treatment of internal disorders and fails to take into account factors outside the persons that produce or maintain an emotional problem. As Zarit (1980) points out:

> Because of the tendency to view old persons as impaired due to their age, excessive use of the medical model and its variants reinforces the likelihood that one will blame a problem on something inside the person and miss those factors in the individual's environment that are influencing or controlling the disturbed behavior (P. 117).

Second, the stress-related view of emotional disorders suggests that nonmedical approaches such as crisis intervention are important aspects of helping older persons cope with life situations that are anxiety-producing. The crisis intervention model is based on the premise that prompt and time-limited intervention, using several treatment modalities, is effective with older persons. Attention is focused on the precipitating factors that result in frustration, anxiety and depression. Helping older persons deal with the crisis in the early stages recognizes that external events are often the sources of emotional distress (Chapter 4).   **Third,** because stress produces a sense of helplessness in older persons that is associated with depression, a problem-solving approach that helps older persons find a reasonable and effective solution to difficulties offers an alternative approach to medical intervention. The problem-solving model can be applied in a wide range of situations that produce confusion, anxiety or depression in older persons and helps them regain control over their lives and restores their sense of worth and self-esteem (Chapter 4).

Fourth, a behavioral approach to emotional disorders is also an effective form of intervention when maladaptive responses to stressful events is the focus of concern. Instead of looking for the cause of the disorder in an underlying cause, this approach is designed to provide older persons with new adaptive responses to stress. By focusing on the specific problems presented by the patient and the context within which they occur, older persons learn to cope with stress (Chapter 4).

Fifth, an emphasis on environmental factors that produces stress argues for the possibility of a social program that can reduce the incidence of emotional disorders among the elderly. Adequate medical care to maintain health can reduce the prevalence of illness and physical disability that is a major cause of depression among the elderly. Providing decent shelter and good nutrition can improve the ability of older persons to deal with stress and maintain mental health and emotional stability.

Sixth, the emphasis on stress as a significant factor in emotional disorders among the elderly strongly suggests that effective intervention efforts need to be broad-based and well-coordinated; that the problem of emotional distress is not the sole concern of any given profession. Medical practitioners, psychiatrists, psychologists, social workers, nurses, psychiatric aides and social planners are all involved in assessing, intervening and solving the problem. The combined efforts of mental health workers can result in a clearer understanding of emotional disorders in later life and lead to more effective modes of treating them.

Summary

Older persons are subjected to many emotional disorders that are found in other age groups: hypochondriasis, anxiety reactions, paranoid states and depression. Some emotional problems and functional psychological dysfunctions are caused by underlying physical or biological factors that require medical intervention. Some emotional difficulties are due to a combination of past life experience and reaction to stressful situations. Other emotional problems are directly or indirectly related to a social environment that fails to provide sufficient economic, psychological and emotional support to older persons. All these factors must be taken into account in planning and implementing an effective form of intervention.

Chapter 3

ASSESSING EMOTIONAL PROBLEMS

Making a careful assessment of the emotional problems of older persons is essential before intervention is undertaken. The assessment process involves the use of psychological tests, physical examinations, psychiatric evaluations and an assessment of the social environment to determine the nature and cause of the client's emotional difficulty. Medical practitioners, psychiatrists, psychologists and social workers contribute information that is helpful in making a comprehensive, multi-dimensional assessment of the client and the social context within which the emotional problem developed.

Conducting the Assessment

Special considerations enter into conducting an assessment when older persons are involved. Among these are the following:

1. Generally, interviews should be shorter than with other age groups, because even healthy elderly patients become fatigued after about 40 minutes. Elderly persons with some brain impairment may not be able to attend for more than 10 minutes and need to be seen repeatedly to obtain sufficient information.
2. Older persons must be given sufficient time to respond to questions and to test items. An emphasis on a speedy response will result in older patients looking less adequate than they would appear in daily life and end in a false perception of their performance.
3. Verbal encouragement and praise should be used to obtain information. Accuracy in gauging the quality of an older person's performance is increased when they receive positive reinforcement.
4. Supplemental information from other sources may be needed to gain an accurate picture of the client's situation and performance. Family members may be consulted to fill in gaps of information

about previous psychiatric treatment, episodes of emotional disturbance or physical illness.
5. Laboratory work should include glucose level and electrolyte assays and other tests needed to explore or explain the presence of clinical symptoms.
6. The assessment should include the result of a general physical examination, a review of illnesses under treatment and a listing of all medication that has been prescribed or is being used by the patient.
7. Results of physical therapy, speech therapy and other adjunct therapies should be noted and evaluated.
8. The assessment should include observations on the current living environment, housing, transportation facilities and the quality of life that is afforded the patient.
9. The findings of the various professionals should be integrated into a form that is useful as a guide to intervention.

The assessment should be complete and incorporate the information and conclusions of all who are involved in the process. Hussian (1981) points out the danger in arriving at a premature decision because the patient is old and appears to be "brain damaged":

> We presently have the ability to make accurate differential statements which can result in complete restoration of the elderly client. Though we are quite limited in our ability to reverse deleterious organic processes, we have the ability to return many clients to an acceptable level of functioning.... By assessing those clients whom we have tagged as "organic" and actively treating their functional problems, we can realize a significant gain in the number of successful outcomes. (P. 121.)

Steps in Comprehensive Assessment

A comprehensive assessment of the emotional problems of older persons involves several steps: (1) a comprehensive physical examination; (2) psychological testing; (3) a psychiatric evaluation; and (4) assessment of the client's social environment.

Physical Examination

An accurate medical examination and diagnosis is essential in assessing emotional disorders in older persons. Medical diagnosis for elderly persons must be thorough, because physiological and biological conditions that relate to an emotional state can be overlooked. A careful geriatric examination prevents undertreatment or overtreatment of symptoms and a tendency to overuse "senile dementia" in making a diagnosis. The medical examination can determine if a specific disease may be the underlying cause of mental dysfunctions or affective disturbances.

A review of the functioning of the client's vital systems is a part of a comprehensive physical examination. During this review, a health history can be obtained, symptoms of disease, including pain, visual problems, sleep habits, appetite and sexual functioning can be illicited. The physical examination may also include a rectal and pelvic examination. Conditions that are especially related to functional ability should be noted, especially impaired vision and hearing. Inquiry about the use of medication, both prescribed and over-the-counter products, should be included in the medical examination. Results of treatment for a previous chronic or acute disease should also be noted.

A laboratory examination is essential for geriatric clients who develop psychopathology and should include a complete blood count, renal, liver and thyroid function studies, electrolytes, chest x-ray and serum concentrations of drugs that the client is taking. If brain damage is suspected, an electro-encephalogram and computerized axial tomography of the head should be completed to establish pathology in this area. Other specific laboratory examinations may also be necessary to arrive at a sound diagnosis. A neurological examination is also essential in making a complete physical assessment of emotional or mental dysfunctions.

Differentiating depression from physical disease, particularly dementia, is especially important, since depression is treatable and many of the dementias are not. In some cases of a severely depressed individual, such a differential diagnosis is difficult because many cognitive changes, primarily deficits in recall and memory, occur in depressed persons. The appearance of cognitive dysfunctioning may lead to a premature diagnosis and an underlying depression may be overlooked as a cause of problems in cognitive functioning. Agitation or an inability to respond to the examiner may lead to a false impression and result in a "missed diagnosis" of a depressive illness in some geriatric clients. Endocrine disorders may present symptoms that are indistinguishable from a major depressive disorder. Depression is also common in clients with chronic renal disease, anemia and brain tumors. Mood changes, lethargy, fatigue, weight loss and sleep disturbance are also seen in systemic diseases or can result from the side effects of psychotropic drugs and anti-hypertensive medication.

Psychological Testing

Various tests have been developed to assess various areas of functioning including orientation, cognition and memory. The most widely used test is the Mental Status Questionnaire consisting of ten questions to determine if the person is oriented to time and place. This instrument is useful as a quick screening device for brain damage (see Figure 1).

FIGURE 1. Short Portable Mental Status Questionnaire (SPMSQ)

Short Portable Mental Status Questionnaire (SPMSW)

1. What is the date today (month/day/year)?
2. What day of the week is it?
3. What is the name of this place?
4. What is your telephone number? (If no telephone, what is your street address?)
5. How old are you?
6. When were you born (month/day/year)?
7. Who is the current president of the United States?
8. Who was the president just before him?
9. What was your mother's maiden name?
10. Subtract 3 from 20 and keep subtracting from each new number you get, all the way down.

    0–2 errors = intact
    3–4 errors = mild intellectual impairment
    5–7 errors = moderate intellectual impairment
    8–10 errors = severe intellectual impairment

Allow one more error if subject had only grade school education.

Allow one fewer error if subject has had education beyond high school.

Allow one more error for blacks, regardless of education criteria.

Source: Duke University. (1978). Center for the Study of Aging and Human Development. Multi-dimensional functional assessment: The OARS methodology. Durham, N.C.: Duke University.

Although this brief mental assessment is useful, caution should be exercised in drawing conclusions based solely on test results. Persons who make errors on the MSQ may be capable of answering questions about their activities, their mood, or their food preferences. Therefore, short tests should be supplemented with other information that may reveal cognitive strengths and capacities that would otherwise go unrecognized.

Several tests have been developed to screen for affective disorders, especially depression. The Zung Self-Rated Depression Scale (Zung, 1965) and the Beck Inventory of Depression are useful in assessing the client's affect (Beck et al., 1961). These scales are shown in Figure 2 and Figure 3.

FIGURE 2. Examples of Scales to Measure Affective Status

Zung Self-Rated Depression Scale

1. I feel downhearted and blue.[a]
2. Morning is when I feel the best.
3. I have crying spells or feel like it.
4. I have trouble sleeping at night.
5. I can eat as much as I used to.
6. I still enjoy sex.
7. I notice that I am losing weight.
8. I have trouble with constipation.
9. My heart beats faster than usual.
10. I get tired for no reason.
11. My mind is as clear as it used to be.
12. I find it easy to do the things I used to.
13. I am restless and can't keep still.
14. I feel hopeful about the future.
15. I am more irritable than usual.
16. I find it easy to make decisions.
17. I feel that I am useful and needed.
18. My life is pretty full.
19. I feel that others would be better off if I were dead.
20. I still enjoy the things I used to do.

[a]For each item, the respondent rates the statement as "a little of the time," "some of the time," "good part of the time," or "most of the time."

Positive well-being is an indication of whether the individual has high or low morale and can assess subjective emotional states. Two instruments are available to measure morale: The Philadelphia Geriatric Center Morale Scale and the Life Satisfaction Index (LSI–A). These morale measurement tests are shown in Figures 4 and 5.

Other tests employed include the Bender Visual-Motor Gestalt test to determine the extent of brain damage by requiring the individual to retain spatial orientation. The person is presented a series of cards with a simple geometric figure on each and is asked to copy each of these figures on a piece of paper. Persons who have organic brain problems will rotate or misplace the figures.

FIGURE 3. Examples of Scales to Measure Affective Status

Modified Beck Depression Inventory[b]

1. I do not feel sad.
   I feel sad.
   I am sad all the time and can't snap out of it.
   I am so sad or unhappy that I can't stand it.
2. I am not particularly discouraged about the future.
3. I do feel like a failure.
4. I get as much satisfaction out of things as I used to.
5. I don't feel particularly guilty.
6. I don't feel I am being punished.
7. I don't feel disappointed in myself.
8. I don't feel I am any worse than anyone else.
9. I don't have thoughts of killing myself.
10. I don't cry any more than usual.
11. I am no more irritated now than I ever am.
12. I have not lost interest in other people.
13. I make decisions about as well as I ever could.
14. I don't worry that I look worse than I used to.
15. I can work about as well as I used to.
16. I can sleep as well as usual.
17. I don't get any more tired than usual.
18. My appetite is no worse than usual.
19. I haven't lost much weight, if any, lately.
20. I am no more worried about my health than usual.
21. I have not noticed any recent change in my interest in sex.

---

[b]Each item has 4–5 responses, representing a range of mood; the respondent picks the one most appropriate. We included all four responses only for item no. 1.

Sources: Zung scale adapted from W.W.K. Zung. (1965). A self-rating depression scale. *Archives of General Psychiatry*, 12, 73–70. Beck inventory from A.T. Beck et al. (1961). An inventory for measuring depression. *Archives of General Psychiatry*, 4, 53–63.

The Wechsler Adult Intelligence Scale is useful in testing the intelligence level of older persons. The WAIS can be given in an abbreviated form in specific areas: information, comprehension, calculation, similarities and vocabulary. Another popular test is the Kent EGY ten-item quick screening instrument for testing intelligence. The Face-Hand Test, originally developed by Bender, determines how well a person can discern simultaneous touch on face and hand. This instrument is useful in distinguishing psychotic individuals from those who are brain damaged.

Several tests have been developed to assess the individual's mental health and personality. The OARS Mental Health Scale, consisting of 15 no/yes questions, is used to screen areas of psychological and emotional problems. Brink and associates have produced the Geriatric Depression

FIGURE 4. Examples of Scales Measuring Subjective Well-Being in the Elderly

Philadelphia Geriatric Center Morale Scale

1. Things keep getting worse as I get older (No)[a]
2. I have as much pep as I did last year. (Yes)
3. How much do you feel lonely? (Not much)
4. Little things bother me more this year. (No)
5. I see enough of my friends and relatives. (Yes)
6. As you get older, you are less useful. (No)
7. If you could live where you wanted, where would you live? (Here)
8. I sometimes worry so much that I can't sleep. (No)
9. As I get older, things are (better, worse, the same) than/as I thought they'd be. (Better)
10. I sometimes feel that life isn't worth living. (No)
11. I am as happy now as I was when I was younger. (Yes)
12. Most days I have plenty to do. (No)
13. I have a lot to be sad about. (No)
14. People had it better in the old days. (No)
15. I am afraid of a lot of things. (No)
16. My health is (good, not so good). (Good)
17. I get mad more than I used to. (No)
18. Life is hard for me most of the time. (No)
19. How satisfied are you with your life today? (Satisfied)
20. I take things hard. (No)
21. A person has to live for today and not worry about tomorrow. (Yes)
22. I get upset easily. (No)

[a] The correct answer, shown in parentheses, is scored one point.

Scale of thirty items to identify the presence of feeling states that are related to depression (1982). Projective tests that elicit spontaneous responses, such as the Rorschach Inkblot Test, provide some information about the individual's personality structure and the unconscious processes underlying his or her behavior. The Minnesota Multiple Personality Inventory measures nine dimensions of personality and may be useful in assessing individuals who are able to complete a paper-and-pencil inventory.

Because few assessment instruments have been rigorously tested for reliability, they should be viewed as aids in making assessments rather than being considered as the primary source for reaching conclusions about the person's emotional state. In short, these instruments must be used with caution and need to be supplemented by other forms of assessment.

FIGURE 5. Examples of Scales Measuring Subjective Well-Being in the Elderly

---

Life Satisfaction Index (LSI–A)

Here are some statements about life in general that people feel differently about. Would you read each statement in the list and, if you agree with it, put a check mark in the space "agree." If you do not agree, put a check mark in the space under "disagree." If you are not sure one way or the other, put a check mark in the space "?."

1. As I grow older, things seem better than I thought they would be. (Agree)
2. I have gotten more of the breaks in life than most of the people I know. (Agree)
3. This is the dreariest time of my life. (Disagree)
4. I am just as happy as when I was younger. (Agree)
5. My life could be happier than it is now. (Disagree)
6. These are the best years of my life. (Agree)
7. Most of the things I do are boring or monotonous. (Disagree)
8. I expect some interesting and pleasant things to happen to me in the future. (Agree)
9. The things I do are as interesting to me as they ever were. (Agree)
10. I feel old and tired. (Disagree)
11. I feel my age, but it doesn't bother me. (Agree)
12. As I look back on my life, I am fairly well satisfied. (Agree)
13. I would not change my past life, even if I could. (Agree)
14. Compared to other people my age, I've made a lot of foolish decisions in my life. (Disagree)
15. Compared to other people my age, I make a good appearance. (Agree)
16. I have made plans for things I'll be doing a month or a year from now. (Agree)
17. When I think back over my life, I didn't get most of the important things I wanted. (Disagree)
18. Compared to other people, I get down in the dumps too often. (Disagree)
19. I've gotten pretty much what I expected out of life. (Agree)
20. In spite of what people say, the lot of the average man is getting worse, not better. (Disagree)

Sources: Moral scale adapted from M.P. Lawton. (1972). The dimensions of morale. In D. Kent R. Kastenbaum, and S. Sherwood (Eds.), *Research planning, and action for the elderly*. New York: Behavioral Publications. Life satisfaction index adapted from R.J. Havinghurst, B.L. Neugarten, and S.S. Tobin. (1961). The measurement of life satisfaction. *Journal of Gerontology*, 16, 134–143.

Psychiatric Evaluation

A psychiatric evaluation provides useful information regarding the patient's cognitive functioning, affective state and personality characteristics.

Exploring mental functioning may identify illogical and incoherent thought processes, ideas of reference, or distortion of reality, including hallucinations and delusions. The presence of these symptoms indicates the nature and extent to which the client may be experiencing temporary or permanent brain damage or brain disease. Observation of the client's mood or affect will identify emotional states such as anxiety and depression, feelings of hopelessness, despair and loneliness. An evaluation of these symptoms will determine the severity of the emotional disorder and the causes of the disturbance.

Depressive thought content, including self-depreciation, statements that reflect irrational guilt and feelings of helplessness, hopelessness, worthlessness, are carefully noted. The psychiatric assessment of depression includes a survey of the symptoms that constitute an affective disorder as defined by the American Psychiatric Association, such as a change in the sleep cycle, usually difficulty in falling asleep, difficulty remaining asleep and early morning awakening. The client may complain of anxiety, weakness or feeling slowed up. Fatigue may prevent the client from undertaking daily tasks and will sometimes not be refreshed after adequate sleep.

Depressed clients feel guilty, have a pronounced sense of failure and blame themselves for perceived inadequacies. Difficulty in concentrating, recent memory, immediate recall and pervasive doubt are often manifested. Severely depressed persons may express suicidal wishes or plans. Since suicide is common among the elderly, the examiner should always ask clients about suicidal ideation.

Depression may result in major physiological consequences due to loss of appetite and withdrawal from food and liquid. In the absence of sufficient fluid, electrolyte problems develop rapidly and can lead to secondary pneumonia or seizures. Because older persons who are depressed become immobile, there is a strong possibility that decubitus ulcers will develop and, if infected, lead to sepsis. For these reasons, depression is more dangerous in older persons than among younger persons.

Because many emotional disorders are related to stressful situations that accompany aging, a psychiatric evaluation should also include an examination of how the client responds to significant losses and the defense mechanisms that the client employs in attempting to ward off anxiety and depression. Among these are denial, projection, fixation, regression, counterphobia, idealization, ritualization, selective memory and selective sensory perception.

Denial is a defense that controls the individual's anxiety about the effects of aging on mental and physical capacity. Older persons often claim that they are still able to do everything they could do when they were young and deny that they need medical attention. When it is used extensively and over a long period of time, denial can have serious consequences because treatment of reversible health problems is postponed or neglected.

Projection is a form of self-defense that older persons may use when they are no longer able to take care of themselves and must depend on others to handle their affairs. Projection takes the form of mistrustful behavior when the individual thinks that other persons are taking advantage of his or her helplessness. Older persons who become highly suspicious and who develop symptoms of paranoid states create difficulties for persons in their immediate environment.

Fixation, or a refusal to accept change, is a common defense against aging. Older persons are often regarded as being stubborn because they resist changing their daily accustomed pattern of living. Avoiding change gives older persons a feeling of security, provides a sense of continuity and helps them maintain their self-identity.

Regression, or a return to earlier levels of adaptation, is often used to explain "childlike" behavior in older persons. This defense mechanism is generally employed when individuals face a crisis that is overwhelming. In most cases, the regressive behavior disappears after the stress diminishes.

Counterphobia is a compelling tendency to look danger in the face and convince oneself that it can be overcome. Older persons are prone to place great value on independence and self-reliance. They may refuse to acknowledge that danger exists and will not accept protection when needed. An older man who is subject to dizziness may insist on climbing a ladder to fix the roof. An older woman who feels a rapid heartbeat when she climbs stairs may insist that she can still do so several times a day to prove that she is not incapacitated.

Idealization is a defense that older persons use when they lose a valued person or place. A wife may idealize her husband after his death in an effort to make her life meaningful. Living in the past is one of the frequent behavior patterns developed by the elderly. A life review may take the form of nostalgia and recalling events that are comforting, give a sense of serenity, pride in accomplishment and satisfaction in having done one's best.

Ritualistic behavior is often used to compensate for a decrease in sensory powers and memory loss. Such rituals include meticulous ways of entering the house, locking doors, certain ways of dressing and undressing and going to bed. Becoming a slave to a certain routine seems senseless to others but may give some older persons a feeling of security.

Selective Memory and Selective Sensory Perception are common forms of defense imaging. Although deficits in memory are usually attributed to brain changes, they may actually have a psychological base. Older persons who do not recall recent events may be tuning out the painful present and dwell on a more happy and satisfying past. A process of "exclusion of stimuli" has been observed in individuals who have hearing problems but seem to hear what they want to hear and can control the input from the environment by using this defense.

Older persons may exploit aging and disability for their own benefit. By appearing totally helpless, they can demand the concern and services of others. They may remain in the hospital when they no longer need medical care because they enjoy the extra attention they receive. Some use aging as a way to avoid complying with social norms and take on a new identity that allows them to engage in behavior that is idiosyncratic but harmless.

A healthy adaptation to aging has been called "responsible dependency" as described by Butler and Lewis: "The concept implies realistic evaluation of when one begins to require help from others and an ability to accept that help with dignity and cooperativeness, rather than denying the need or abusing the opportunity to be dependent. Insight includes the willingness and ability to substitute available satisfactions for losses incurred. It is the most widely used and successful adaptation found among older people" (1977, pp. 48–49).

Older persons who have a history of prior affective disorders are likely to present the symptoms of classical depression. They usually have had difficulty resolving conflicts about dependency and coping with hostility in the past. Many older persons tend to regress when confronted with stress and are likely to display strong dependency strivings. To some extent, regressive behavior is natural and a universal reaction to loss and stress. In late life, the tendency to regress is exacerbated because the physical and psychological resources of the person are depleted and less energy is available to cope with stress.

Assessing the Social Environment

An assessment of the client's social environment is aimed at exploring and identifying factors that contribute to the client's emotional distress.

This assessment focuses on three principal areas: physical aspects of the environment, the client's social network, and the client's family.

The Physical Environment. The physical environment includes the natural and man-made resources that are essential to survival, including shelter and social services. A study of the living arrangements of the older person should address these questions: Does the living arrangement meet his or her physical needs? What changes should be made in the present arrangement that would improve living standards? Is the community and neighborhood safe for older persons? Is there easy access to public transportation? Are there nearby stores where the patient can shop? Is the area in which the patient lives relatively quiet and free from congestion?

The assessment should also include a survey of facilities that the patient needs, such as a medical clinic, mental health center or day-care facility. Older persons have difficulty in using these services because they are often far removed from where they live; ready access to these facilities vastly improves the likelihood that these important services will be used by older persons. Even more important is the reception that older persons receive when they seek professional help from mental health and welfare personnel. Because older persons are especially sensitive to negative reactions from others, these services should provide an atmosphere that reflects respect and support for the aging.

The Social Network. The social network refers to important persons in the client's environment: relatives, friends and neighbors. A social network meets the need of older persons for valued interaction with others and prevents them from becoming socially isolated and lonely. The social network also gives older persons a sense of identity, reaffirms their self-worth and is a strong defense against depression. Religious and ethnicities are especially valued among older persons and provide not only a sense of security but are a source of pride and increased self-esteem.

Social networks also serve as a mutual aid system that helps older persons cope with stress. When they have no social network to call upon in time of crisis or need, older persons become anxious and depressed. Finding ways to link the patient to others who can provide emotional and practical support is a legitimate concern of all mental health workers. Therefore, an assessment should include a survey of community resources that can assist older persons, such as protective services from a special arm of the police department, social service workers and community volunteer agencies. By using these services, older persons can develop an ability to negotiate their environment and can begin to gain more control over their lives.

Family Relationships. A crucial factor in assessing the emotional problems of older persons involves the individual's relationship to family members—to the spouse and to adult children. An emotional difficulty such as severe depression has a profound impact on family members and can change family structure. For example, if the wife becomes seriously depressed, the husband may be called upon to play a highly supportive and nurturing role. If the father becomes mentally confused or emotionally disturbed, the executive and managerial roles that he normally plays will have to be taken over by his wife or some other family member.

In assessing the effect of an emotional problem on the marriage relation, the following questions should be addressed: How does the marital partner respond to the needs of the client? Has the marital bond been strong in the past, and will it continue to remain strong? Does the marital partner have the physical, mental and emotional resources needed to meet the demands placed on him or her by the emotional or mental difficulty of the spouse?

An emotional illness also has a significant impact on the relationship between the parents and their adult children. A parent's emotional dysfunction increases dependence on an adult son or daughter. In some families, this transition to a new relationship can be made smoothly, but often family members have difficulty resolving the problems of dependency and care-giving that are associated with such a crisis.

The relationship between the client and adult children needs to be explored, and the following questions should be addressed: How do the adult children respond to the emotional problems of the aging parent? Does the patient's current problem raise issues that have been troublesome in the past? Are the siblings united in their opinion as to "what should be done"? Does the client have conflicting feelings toward one or more of the adult children? Do issues of sibling rivalry stand in the way of helping the patient recover or improve? What resources can the children offer that will be helpful?

The following outline suggests the content of a multi-dimensional assessment:

ASSESSMENT OUTLINE

I. Presented Problems
  A. Physical functioning
    1. acute or chronic disease
    2. systemic malfunctioning
    3. biochemical imbalance
    4. physical impairment
    5. organic brain disease
  B. Cognitive functioning
    1. incoherent or illogical thinking
    2. delusional, obsessive thoughts
    3. deficits in immediate recall or long-term memory
    4. disorientation to time and place
    5. mental confusion
  C. Affective functioning
    1. apathy and indifference
    2. feelings of guilt and self-blame
    3. sense of loneliness and isolation
    4. expressions of helplessness or hopelessness
    5. withdrawal from social contacts
    6. anxiety or agitation
    7. perception of self
  D. Responses to stress
    1. denial
    2. fixation
    3. regression
    4. counterphobia
    5. idealization
    6. ritualistic behavior

II. Social Environment Assessment
  A. Physical characteristics
    1. living arrangements
    2. financial resources
    3. health services
    4. protective services
  B. Social network
    1. relation to family members
    2. relation to peers

3. ethnic groups
             4. religious groups
             5. informal groups
          C. Family relationships
             1. relation between marital partners
             2. relation between parent and adult children
             3. financial resources of family members
             4. changes in role responsibilities
III. Summary
     A. Physical functioning
     B. Mental functioning
     C. Emotional reactions to stress
     D. Physical environment
     E. Social network
     F. Family relationships

The following case illustrates how an assessment can be stated in a brief form.

Presented Problems. Mr. J, age 72, complained of difficulty in remembering and some minor confusion in orientation. He expressed a fear that he was deteriorating intellectually and also was concerned about a drastic loss of interest in sexual activity. He felt depressed, slept more than usual and tended to withdraw from social contacts. His speech was sometimes hesitant, and he had difficulty concentrating.

Physical Examination. A physical examination indicated that Mr. J had a history of good health. Laboratory tests were negative, and there was no evidence of physiological dysfunctions. Hearing and visual functions were normal. Family health history showed no hereditary diseases.

Psychological Testing. A complete battery of psychological tests were administered to determine the presence of organic brain disorders, with special reference to the presence of Alzheimer's disease. The tests showed negative in respect to organic brain dysfunctions, and memory impairment was well within normal limits. Cognitive function was above average, but there were definite findings of moderate disturbance in affect.

Psychiatric Evaluation. Psychiatric evaluation showed symptoms of depression including loss of libidinal interest, lack of psychic energy, and difficulty in prolonged concentration. Laboratory tests for bi-polar depression were negative. Brain scan test results were negative in respect to brain disease or brain damage. The depressive symptoms were regarded as moderate, and suicidal ideation was absent.

Social Assessment. Mr. J is able to care for himself without assistance, but his inability to communicate his feelings to his wife and his loss of sexual interest has had a dilatory effect on his marriage. He relates his depressed feelings to his retirement after a successful career as a university professor at age 70. He had been intellectually active and had written four books in the five years prior to his retirement. He had been a popular instructor and was respected by his colleagues. Mr. J and his wife continue to live near the university. Mrs. J is self-employed and conducts a successful small business enterprise. They are financially secure and neither have serious health problems. Mr. J's unmarried adult son and daughter maintain contact with their parents.

Summary and Recommendations. Mr. J's emotional reaction to retirement and the loss of an important social role as educator and author are the problems that require attention. His self-esteem and sense of usefulness have been significantly altered and have resulted in a moderate reactive depression. He is in good health, has above-average intelligence and has not been mentally impaired, although his cognitive processes have been slowed by his depression. His health history indicates a favorable prognosis, and he indicates a strong desire to overcome his emotional problem.

Recommendations. The administration of antidepressant medication is indicated to relieve the depression, with supportive therapy as an adjunct to aid in a complete recovery. Mr. J's response to medication will be carefully monitored by the psychiatrist to determine if it is effective in alleviating symptoms of difficulty in concentration and loss of energy as the depression is brought under control. Counseling sessions with a social worker will be scheduled as needed to provide psychological support and restore Mr. J's self-confidence and improve his social functioning. Mr. J's wife will also be included in counseling to relieve her anxiety about her husband's illness and to provide psychological support for her.

Planning Intervention

A multi-dimensional assessment leads to a consideration of the goal of intervention and choosing an approach that will be effective in achieving the goal. The following outline suggests the goals of major treatment models that can be useful in helping older persons cope with emotional distress. Although each approach involves specific techniques, intervention can often consist of a combination of treatment methods. Intervention should be flexible and tailored to meet the special needs of a particular individual.

Supportive Therapy is a non-specific form of helping that is aimed at maintaining the client's current functioning and may also include efforts designed to help clients make a satisfactory adaptation to loss and change. Supportive therapy can be useful in a wide range of situations with persons who are severely incapacitated as well as those who are only marginally impaired. Supportive intervention may focus on attitude and self-image or may include providing solutions to practical problems or management of everyday affairs.

Behavioral Therapy aims at affecting changes in the behavior of patients through the use of reinforcement techniques and teaching new skills that will improve functioning. In some respects, behavior modification is aimed at cure, i.e. eliminating a behavioral problem. However, it has some value in helping older persons adapt to new or stressful situations. Behavior modification is also targeted at those persons who display depression or anxiety and problems in socialization.

Cognitive Therapy aims at changing irrational or maladaptive thought processes and can be used in treating depression or in helping older persons cope with loss. The focus is on ways of thinking that lead to unproductive behavior or emotional distress. Cognitive therapy is targeted to a wide range of emotional problems, including reactions to stress or delusional affect.

Crisis Intervention is aimed at helping older persons cope with emotionally hazardous events that produce anxiety and depressive feelings. The goal is primarily adaptation to a changed situation and may be used in working with terminally ill patients and their families or helping older persons cope with the death of a spouse. The focus includes affective and cognitive functions and usually involves psychological support in helping the patient cope with the impact of a crisis.

Task-Centered Casework involves the development of tasks that lead to the resolution of problems in interpersonal relations, dissatisfaction in social relations, decisionmaking problems, reactive emotional distress and inadequate resources. Attention is focused on helping clients resolve specific problems and enabling them to pursue a course of action that will diminish or eliminate their emotional discomfort. The caseworker actively engages in helping clients elect a target problem, design tasks that will eliminate it and encourage clients to complete tasks.

Family Therapy is aimed at resolving problems in the relationship between older persons and their adult children or difficulties between the husband and wife. The goal is primarily adaptation to changes in relationship that come with aging. The focus is on helping family members communicate and resolve the underlying difficulties with which they are trying to cope. The target population includes older persons' families who need professional help in dealing with a wide range of problems, including decisions about long-term care, conflict between adult siblings or between parents and their adult children. It may also include older couples who are experiencing difficulty in resolving marital problems that relate to the aging process.

Group Therapy may be used to achieve a variety of goals, some of which are adaptive and others are curative or enriching. Curative approaches are achieved through group psychotherapy. Adaptive group approaches focus on cognitive loss and may also be designed to help older persons learn new behavior patterns. Enrichment groups focus on the development of self-identity and self-worth and the continued growth of older persons. The socialization that group therapy offers is a supportive measure that also enables older persons to maintain or improve their social functioning. The targets of group therapy vary. Some groups are aimed at helping older persons who have cognitive problems. Others are aimed at those who have behavioral problems. Self-support groups are formed around common problems that older people face, such as loss of health, death of a spouse, or social isolation.

How these various approaches can be used to help older persons cope with emotional problems is the subject of the chapters that follow.

Chapter 4

SOCIAL CASEWORK INTERVENTION

In the course of its history, social work has developed several models of intervention that are applicable to working with older persons. Among these approaches are supportive casework, crisis intervention, and task-centered casework. Recently, two models based on social learning theory have become recognized as additional forms of social work intervention: behavior modification and cognitive therapy. Although each of these approaches have distinguishing characteristics, they are closely related and can be integrated in helping older persons cope with emotional problems.

Supportive Casework

Supportive casework practice has long been recognized as a useful approach in helping people cope with a wide range of situations and can be effective in working with older persons who present emotional problems. This model of intervention is not designed to bring about fundamental changes in the client's personality through the uncovering of internalized conflicts. However, it is appropriate in working with older persons who have suffered loss in ego functioning or who are threatened by an external event. Older persons are likely to experience simultaneous losses: the death of friends, afflictions of the body and mind, loss of social relationships, occupation, role status and possessions. The impact of these accumulated losses produces severe stress and can precipitate emotional breakdown. Moreover, these losses occur in the later years when individuals have less psychic and physical energy to cope with problems. Therefore, a supportive relationship that helps older persons cope with loss is a critical component of the helping process.

Goal of Supportive Casework. Supportive casework is based on the view that aging involves a depletion of resources to cope with loss and regards regression as a non-pathological defense among elderly persons. Older persons are often dependent on others and must rely on them to sustain them when their own physical and emotional resources are insufficient. Regression is therefore seen as a legitimate defense and accepted as a natural outgrowth of the relationship that develops in the course of working with older persons. In short, the worker lends part of his or her ego strengths to the older client when there are manifest breakdowns in instinctual drives or a disturbance in emotional and mental functioning.

The supportive approach draws heavily on the effectiveness of therapeutic relationship in effective intervention, especially in working with older persons. Helen Perlman (1970) refers to relationship as "the most potent and dynamic power for influence" and points out that a relationship that reflects caring and respect is essential regardless of the theoretical model of helping. "The need for these peculiarly human forms of nourishment is intensified at times of vulnerability, helplessness and stress," she writes. "So it may be expected that a person who finds himself resourceless and empty-handed in the face of a problem will need and want connection with someone who combines caring for him with social power and authority to help him" (p. 150).

The supportive relationship is characterized by a combination of concern and acceptance of the client with a capacity to act effectively on the client's behalf. The effectiveness of the supportive approach depends largely on how empathy, warm acceptance and caring are demonstrated by the helping person. During the early phase of intervention, depending on the worker will be seen as appropriate. As treatment progresses, the client gradually gains confidence in his ability to function independently by identifying with the worker, can incorporate constructive ways of solving problems and terminate the helping process.

Supporting Techniques. Among the techniques employed in supportive casework are: reassurance, validation, positive feedback, acceptance, catharsis, education and provision of concrete services.

Reassurance includes expressions that recognize the individual's capacities and show respect for the client's feelings and needs.

Validation gives positive feedback to clients and demonstrates that they have valuable assets and are regarded as competent persons.

Acceptance indicates to clients that they are considered worthy persons regardless of their social status or personal characteristics.

These techniques involve what Hollis describes as "reflective communications in which the worker attempts to sustain the client through expressions of interest, sympathy and understanding, desire to help, confidence in the client and acceptance of him." The effect of these sustaining communications is to reduce anxiety or increase self-confidence.

Catharsis, ventilation of anger, frustration and hopelessness, are important aspects of supportive casework, especially in helping clients cope with the loss of a loved friend or relative. Older persons are especially vulnerable to anxiety and depression in periods of transition; they often feel lonely and confused by traumatic life events. The presence of someone with whom they can share their feelings is extremely important. As Butler (1975) points out, the act of listening is intrinsically therapeutic: "One function of mental health specialists which has direct application to work with older people is cultivation of the act of listening. The so-called garrulousness of old people and their wish to hold on so tenaciously to someone's attention is a social symptom related to their loneliness. Patience, listening and simply spending meaningful time with them are of great therapeutic value" (p. 230).

Supplying information, providing concrete services and offering protective services are additional measures employed in supportive casework.

Education includes imparting information, giving advice or guidance to older clients and their families in considering alternative solutions to a specific problem. Older persons who have undergone loss in cognitive functioning or who are experiencing a high level of anxiety or depression can benefit from this form of support that compensates for such deficiencies. Advice and guidance are used sparingly and are offered only if clients are unable to make decisions on their own behalf and need to turn to a professional person in whom they can trust.

Providing Concrete Service. Helping clients seek out and use needed concrete services such as health care, financial assistance, nutritional services, recreational programs and homemaker services is an important adjunct in supportive casework. The primary objective is to steer clients to existing services that can meet a specific need. Clients are enabled to negotiate steps they must take to obtain the service of a specific agency or social welfare program. If older persons are able to seek out and use these resources on their own, they are encouraged to do so, but in some instances, the worker may take over for clients to ensure that they receive the help to which they are entitled.

Protective Services. Social casework with older persons who need protection has become a matter of increasing concern. A critical factor in the use of protective services centers around the question of what standards are to be applied in determining if protection is needed and serves the best interest of the client. Various factors enter into making such a determination: the ability of the individual to care for himself, physically and financially; whether he has the mental capacity to survive without supervision; and whether he will be exploited or neglected if protection is not available.

Associated with these problems are other questions: Who should assume responsibility for offering protection? Who has the right to intervene when a crucial decision must be made and the client has the capacity to do so? Social workers are often involved in these knotty problems. Although exercising authority in behalf of the client can present a dilemma, a supportive approach does involve the worker in protective measures to prevent neglect and serious deterioration of older persons.

Planning Placement. Supportive casework service is indicated when aged persons must make a change in living arrangements because they are no longer able to care for themselves. Separation anxiety is common among the elderly when they are forced to leave familiar surroundings for a new, unknown place and are deprived of a supporting social network. There is a growing recognition that making a major shift from independence and self-reliance to becoming dependent on others is a difficult transition for older persons and for their families. It usually involves strong emotional reactions from family members and evokes feelings of failure and guilt for all who are concerned about the aged family member. Approaching the need for a change in the care of an older person, therefore, requires special sensitivity to the complex psychological factors involved in making a major change. A supportive relation to the client and the family can ease the pain in carrying out a suitable placement plan, helping the client and family members consider alternative plans, and assisting them in choosing a placement that takes into account the client's needs. The process involved in accomplishing this goal is discussed in Chapter 6.

Application to Practice: An Outline. Application of supportive casework in helping older persons cope with emotional problems is summarized in the following outline:

Casework with Individuals:

> Supportive casework is used as a form of psychotherapy in the management of reactive depression, often in conjunction with the administration of antidepressant medication.

Supportive casework is helpful in the control of anxiety reactions due to lack of resources or emotional distress associated with environmental stress.

The techniques of supportive casework are especially useful in helping older persons cope with losses such as major physical disabilities, terminal illness and impending death.

Casework with Families:

Supportive casework is also used to help the families of older persons by providing the following services:

Helping families plan long-term or emergency care for an aged parent or spouse.

Helping family members become actively and constructively involved in providing psychological support and financial assistance in time of crisis.

Enabling families to accept the physical or mental decline of a loved person and offer emotional support when death is inevitable.

Supportive Techniques in Group Therapy:

The techniques of supportive therapy (reassurance, validation, acceptance, catharsis, education) are used extensively in group therapy programs for the elderly in the following ways:

Using the support of group members to improve self-image and build self-confidence.

Providing opportunities for group members to express feelings openly without fear or guilt.

Supporting group members in finding solutions to common problems.

Evaluation of Supportive Casework. The principles and techniques of supportive casework have significant implications for working with older persons who present emotional problems.

First, the emphasis this model places on the casework relationship as an essential component of the therapeutic process is especially applicable to work with the elderly who are extremely sensitive to rejection, have feelings of low self-esteem and lack self-confidence. A supportive relationship manifests concern, empathy and positive regard. Because most emotional problems of older persons are associated with significant losses, the supportive model points the direction that the helping process takes to enable clients to regain a sense of mastery over their lives and restore their self-confidence through the therapeutic relationship.

Edinburg (1985) points out that a supportive approach is especially well-suited to working with older persons and should not be regarded as a "second-rate" form of psychotherapy.

> Working to help individuals maintain their functioning at the highest level, cope with physical and mental losses, handle death of a spouse or prepare for their own death should be viewed as a highly complex form of intervention and considered extremely important in the mental health of the aged (P. 155).

Second, the supportive casework calls attention to loss as the underlying factor in emotional problems of aging. The supportive approach suggests that sustaining and restitution measures are essential in helping older persons cope with depression, anxiety and other affective disorders, as well as in cases that involve cognitive and physical impairment. Indeed, emotional reactions to cognitive or physical deficiencies are seen as the problem that requires attention. Sustaining clients who undergo such losses is therefore regarded as a form of restitution, in that the individual is able to survive the trauma and is restored to a feeling of adequacy and self-worth.

Third, a supportive approach places emphasis on accepting disordered affect, irrational and negative attitudes of older persons and the need for the worker to engage in an empathetic response to their behavior. Dependency is seen as an important factor in working with older persons. Turner (1978) suggests that dependency creates anxiety for the clients as well as the worker:

> The attribute of dependency is an important concept underlying the therapeutic endeavors of the social worker. It can be a powerful adjunct to such endeavors as well as a potential detriment. As a social being, man becomes aware of his need for and his dependency on others. This becomes the source of both anxiety and uncertainty. Anxiety about the dependability of others and the adequacy of resources to meet one's needs (P. 24).

The supportive casework approach is effective in minimizing anxiety by supplying older persons with concrete services and resources and simultaneously providing a sustaining relationship on which they can rely.

Fourth, the supportive model places importance on adaptation to the aging process as a core concept. In large measure, this view of helping stems from the theory that human development consists of completing tasks that are commensurate with various life stages. An emotional problem is seen as an unsatisfactory resolution of conflicts that need to be addressed. Erikson (1963) suggests that the issue which individuals must confront in late life involves despair on the one hand or integrity on the other hand. The resolution of this dilemma is germane to the purpose of a supportive casework approach to the emotional problems of older clients. The goal is to help persons overcome despair and achieve a sense of fulfillment and satisfaction in old age. Each individual is seen as a valued person who has potentials even in late life, and therapy is directed toward helping them achieve integrity, a sense of satisfaction, and feelings of self-worth.

Finally, supportive casework recognizes that an emotional problem must be seen in its social context; that the person and the social environment are reciprocally interrelated. An emotional problem involves the reaction of a specific individual to a specific situation. As psychosocial casework practice suggests, intervention must take both into account. Supportive casework sustains the person who must cope with environment stress but also gives attention to eliminating the source of stress. Sherman (1981) points out that this person-in-situation approach to helping older people has great merit and warns that the role of the mental health worker can "all too easily become that of technical expert and virtuoso with a bag of scientific techniques and procedures, which can lead to inadequate attention to the pervasive social, medical and economic needs of many elderly individuals."

Task-Centered Casework

Task-centered casework is a form of short-term intervention that helps clients solve problems by developing and carrying out specific tasks to overcome presented difficulties (Reid and Epstein, 1977). Intervention involves several stages: (1) identifying and classifying the client's target problem; (2) developing tasks the client is committed to carry out; (3) implementing the tasks; and (4) reviewing the client's progress in solving the target problem.

Selecting a Target Problem. Problems perceived by clients are elicited in the initial interview, and the target problem is identified. The target problem is one that the client is most interested in solving and is the focus of intervention. To determine and define the target problem, the client and worker engage in a structured process that includes the following steps:

1. **Eliciting All Problems with Which the Client is Concerned.** This will probably result in a list of four or five items around which the client is experiencing discomfort and are problems that remain unresolved.

2. **Defining the Problem in Specific Behavioral Terms.** A general description of a problem is not useful as a basis for developing tasks. For example, "being depressed" should be described in behavioral terms such as "has no appetite," "does not talk with others," "seldom leaves the house" or other specific forms of behavior.

3. **Establishing Priority Among Presented Problems.** Clients are sometimes ready to decide which problem should receive the most attention and can rate them in order of importance. In some cases, more than one problem is selected, especially if several are interrelated.

4. **Specifying the Problem and Bringing It into Manageable Limits.** The task-centered approach is goal-directed and there is an urgency about identifying a specific desired outcome as early as possible, and tasks can be developed and carried out. To do so, the problem must be relatively circumscribed and clearly defined from the outset.

Developing Tasks. After the target problem has been selected and clearly specified, tasks need to be developed that will result in a solution to the problem. For example, older persons who are depressed will often focus on a somatic complaint as their chief problem, such as inability to sleep, fatigue or restlessness. A specific complaint may be selected by the client as more important than other problems, and the client may decide to undergo a complete physical examination as a first step to solving the problem. The client may be motivated to carry out this task but would not be willing to consult a psychiatrist about an emotional concern. Moreover, the task is relatively simple and can be carried out quickly.

The task should be one that will be useful in accomplishing a given objective. In the case of a depressed client who is experiencing some somatic discomfort, the search for a cause and remedy of the distressing symptoms may be quite legitimate. In any case, having the results of a complete physical examination would be an important step in solving one of the presented problems and would be useful in planning other tasks that relate to the client's emotional state.

Overloading the client with multiple tasks should be avoided, especially with older persons who have limited energy available. However, a sequence of tasks may be laid out to give further direction to the client. For example, if the physical examination does not result in finding a medical reason for the fatigue, then other tasks will be considered, but these do not need to be defined until the original task has been completed. New tasks can be formulated as the need arises or as the client accomplishes those that have been assigned and agreed to earlier.

Establishing Incentives and Rationale. Clients need to believe that the performance of the task will pay off in solving the problem. If the client is uncertain that benefits will be gained by carrying out the task, steps need to be taken to explain the positive consequences. If this fails, modifying the task or developing an alternative one is also possible. Or, the client may be asked to consider the consequences of **not** performing the task and letting the problem go unsolved. Consistent praise for the client's efforts is also a strong incentive to complete a task and encourage the client to continue in working on the problem.

Simulation, Rehearsal and Guided Practice. Enabling clients to approach unfamiliar situations with confidence and competence through the use of simulation has proven effective in several modes of intervention. Clients can carry out tasks under controlled conditions, engage in role playing and rehearse tasks before attempting them in actuality. Role-playing episodes can be modified and repeated several times, giving clients an opportunity to evaluate their performance. Guided practice differs from role playing, in that the client actually performs the task, with the therapist serving as tutor or coach. These techniques are commonly employed in behavior therapy groups to develop new responses to stress-producing situations.

Analyzing Obstacles. During the implementation of the task, obstacles to performance may arise. Some obstacles are socially determined and cannot be directly overcome. But some obstacles are dysfunctional beliefs which interfere with completing or undertaking a given task. These invalid beliefs can be challenged by requiring the client to test them in reality. Consistent reassurance that expresses confidence in the client's competence is also an approach that enables them to overcome obstacles and carry out an assigned task.

Reviewing Tasks. A task review is essential to hold clients responsible for carrying out tasks that they have agreed to undertake and usually takes place at the beginning of each session. The review gives clients an opportunity to discuss difficulties they are encountering and can lead to a reconsideration of the tasks or reinforcing the client's motivation to continue in completing the task. The review process continues until a satisfactory formulation is agreed to and eventually carried out. The final review comes when the time limit has been reached and service is to be terminated. Attention is focused on determining what has been accomplished, planning how the client can continue working on the target problem by applying what has been learned.

Application to Practice

The task-centered approach can be used in helping older persons cope with emotional problems that are related to stressful life situations that have been identified by Reid, including problems in interpersonal relations, social relations, making decisions, reactive emotional distress and inadequate resources.

Problems in Interpersonal Relationships. Conflict between older persons and their adult children is not uncommon for many families. Parents may expect more emotional or financial support than their children are prepared to offer. Or parents may resent their children's overly solicitous and protective attitude that makes them appear to be inadequate or incompetent to manage their own lives. If the struggle between older persons and their adult children goes unresolved, the damage to the parent-child relationship may not be repaired and continues to cause serious emotional distress and isolation for aged parents.

Dissatisfaction in Social Relations. Older persons tend to become socially isolated and lonely. The feeling of loneliness may be brought on by the death of the marital partner. Living alone can have profound emotional consequences for older persons who need intimacy and companionship. Despondency sets in and suicidal thoughts may emerge unless the surviving spouse finds some other sources of social contact and emotional fulfillment.

Barriers to social contact often involve environmental factors that play an important part in social isolation. Older persons are sometimes forced to live in unsafe neighborhoods or unfamiliar surroundings. Transportation facilities may be unavailable or too costly to allow some older persons to visit friends or attend social events. Not knowing about special programs especially designed to meet the needs of older persons may also account for social isolation.

Loss of health and difficulty in moving about can also be the source of isolation and loneliness for older persons who have deteriorated physically. But there are also psychological barriers to socialization that may pose serious problems. Some older people want to have more opportunities to interact with others but are reluctant to initiate social contacts because they fear that their overtures will be rejected. Loss of self-esteem and feelings of little worth may be found to be the underlying problem that requires attention.

Difficulty in Meeting Expectations. Older persons vary in regard to what they expect from themselves. At one extreme are those who feel that old age is a time for withdrawal from life. They assume a passive stance, tend to avoid new undertakings and begin to limit their contact with the outside world. Many who assume this passive attitude toward aging have never actually been very aggressive in achieving goals during their earlier life, and some are quite comfortable in continuing this pattern as they make the transition to old age.

On the other extreme are those who are disappointed in what they have achieved during their lifetime. They may become bitter because they have been cheated out of opportunities or thwarted in their ambition by force of circumstances. Or they may blame themselves for not having accomplished more or failing to use their talents more effectively. As Robert Butler points out, much important information about an older person's state of mind can be revealed in a life review that explores hitherto unexpressed feelings about one's self and others.

Exploring this area with patients can often clarify the source of emotional discomfort. Wives may regret that they were unfaithful to their husbands and express guilt because they neglected their children. Men may feel that they were too engrossed in their work and careers and failed to provide for the emotional needs of their families. Everyone probably feels that in one respect or another he has not completely lived up to his own expectations or those of others. When death approaches, these thoughts may become obsessive and are extremely discomforting. To reveal them is, in itself, painful. Therefore, an assessment of how the patient perceives his life, how he regards his accomplishments and how useful his life has been can lead to helping him deal with feelings of guilt or failure.

Difficulty in Making Decisions. When called upon to make decisions, some older persons experience great anxiety due to their lack of confidence in their ability to make sound judgments even in day-to-day affairs of minor importance. A high level of anxiety interferes with their ability to take a course of action and results in prolonged procrastination that aggravates the problem and increases their emotional discomfort. Family members often get involved in the patient's inability to act and are tempted to take matters into their own hands if they become sufficiently frustrated and impatient as the indecisiveness continues unabated.

A study of the personality pattern of older persons who are indecisive usually provides some insight into the problem. There is a strong likelihood that the individual has always had problems with decision making and tends to persist in being overly cautious as he or she grows older. Some elderly persons are reluctant to make a decision because they fear the consequence of their action will be irreversible and are afraid to trust their own judgment. Some are inclined to drift, permitting circumstances to determine what will occur. Others will abrogate their autonomy and prefer that others make decisions for them.

Reaction to Emotional Stress. Older persons experience great emotional distress when their marital partner becomes seriously incapacitated or dies. An exploration of the feelings that the loss evoked will be helpful in determining the source of emotional discomfort. The most common component is guilt. A temporary state of mental confusion is also present in most cases, but this will dissipate within a relatively short time. If denial, guilt or confusion continues to prevent the individual from carrying out normal functions and responsibilities, more intensive investigation and evaluation will be necessary to determine if the emotional trauma presents serious problems in adapting to the loss.

A severe loss may trigger a depression and can result in suicidal thinking or acts. The possibility of a depressive state should therefore be taken into account. If the loss continues to preoccupy the person to the exclusion of other matters, or if the individual shows marked changes in behavior or mood, a psychiatric evaluation is necessary to determine the older person's emotional and mental state.

Behavioral Changes. A wide range of behavioral problems are found among older persons. In some cases, the bizarre nature of the behavior indicates a loss of control due to brain damage, and a careful neurological and mental examination is indicated to determine the nature and extent of the disorder. The patient's family will usually be aware of changes in both the thinking and behavioral patterns and can supply information that is useful in making an evaluation of the patient's condition. Firsthand observation also provides a basis for making preliminary judgments about the patient's mental status, such as orientation to time and place, memory and coherent thought.

Certain symptoms may also indicate the presence of a depressive illness. Disturbed sleep patterns and insomnia are frequently associated with depression. Weight loss and lack of appetite are also early signs of a possible depression. Medical symptoms such as a variety of aches and pains that cannot be diagnosed are also indications that the patient is undergoing severe emotional stress that requires extensive psychological and psychiatric evaluation.

Inadequate Financial or Social Resources. Although the passage of the Social Security Act now provides financial support for older Americans, a disproportionate number of persons aged 65 or older still live below the poverty line. The fear of not having enough money to pay rent, buy food and pay for expensive medical care haunts many older persons. Those who are fortunate enough to have a home and are protected by law from being evicted can fare better than those who have no assurance that they will have a suitable place to live. Older persons who have no sizeable savings on which they can depend are very vulnerable to emotional distress and are constantly anxious about their future. Some will eventually join the ranks of the homeless and undergo the severe stress that comes with trying to survive without a permanent place to live, being forced to stand in soup lines as panhandlers on the streets. Many older persons are unable to withstand the rigors of homelessness and rapidly deteriorate physically, mentally and emotionally.

More and more older persons have no close relatives or family members to whom they can turn in time of adversity. They are concerned about who will take care of them when their health fails and they are no longer able to take care of themselves. Even if they have some contact with adult children or other relatives, there is a limit to what these persons can provide. Moving in with an adult son or daughter may not be possible or advisable, and the security that the extended family once provided is missing in contemporary life.

The ultimate fear of older persons is that they will be abandoned and become socially isolated. Too often, such is the case. A deep feeling of loneliness is part of the daily life of many older citizens. Depression eventually saps their energy and a sense of hopelessness causes them to withdraw even farther into themselves. Some will be overwhelmed by depression and take their own lives.

Evaluation of Task-Centered Casework

Task-centered casework does not conform to any formal body of theory. It proceeds on the premise that short-term models of intervention are likely to be more effective than those that involve extended periods of time, because clients are highly motivated to work toward a solution of problems during the early phase of intervention. Reid and Epstein (1972) suggest that placing limitations on duration of helping "forces a concentration on achievable goals, leads to a better planning in use of time available, and stimulates both practitioner and client to greater effort" (p. 92).

Because older clients are usually not amenable to extended treatment, time-limited, short-term intervention is well-suited to meet their needs. They may be involved in repeated short-term therapy as the need arises and can re-enter the helping process again when new problems emerge or when discomfort impels them to become engaged in seeking relief from depression or anxiety (Carmicon, 1977).

Solving problems within a well-defined structure as outlined by Reid and Epstein can have special value in working with older persons because they are more comfortable when they have a clear understanding of how intervention will proceed. The model also defines the role that clients are to play in the solution of problems and provides an opportunity for them to determine what they want to gain. The combination of a defined structure for intervention and freedom of clients to determine specific desired outcomes provides a framework that can readily be adapted to the problems of older persons. Clients are aware that treatment is aimed at certain specific problems and are assured that the intervention will be confined to certain limits. The objectives of traditional approaches are somewhat difficult to communicate. The more limited goals and tighter structure that characterize short-term treatment are perhaps better understood and therefore more readily accepted by the elderly.

The caseworker plays a more directive role in task-centered practice than in other forms of casework intervention. Considerable importance is placed on structuring and attention is focused on a limited area that is of concern to the client. The caseworker holds the client to the performance of a task and must resist the temptation of shifting attention to other problem areas or to dysfunctional behavior that the client does not choose as target problems. These limitations may not be acceptable to caseworkers who have more ambitious aims in treatment and regard the limits imposed by the model as too restrictive. However, the task-centered approach is based on the premise that casework can be effective only when the target problem is one that the client expresses a willingness to work on and can do something about. Therefore, the worker is limited to helping clients resolve target problems.

The task-centered approach to problems of reactive emotional distress places emphasis on the ability of the client to take action that deals with the cause of depression or anxiety. A general or profuse state of emotional disturbance is not regarded as a suitable target problem. It is considered a target problem only if the emotional distress is related to a specific event or set of circumstances that can be clearly identified, such as the death of a family member, loss of status, or illness. If the problem can be understood as relating to such losses, the client can act in ways that will reduce his distress. The caseworker assists the client in developing tasks that will achieve the desired outcome and augment the client's efforts to carry them out.

Complaints of inexplicable anxiety, depression or affective disorders may at first appear to be inappropriate problems for a task-centered approach. However, on closer inspection, they may turn out to be clearly related to social and environmental factors that are producing discomfort and emotional distress. If the client and worker succeed in determining causes of emotional distress, the target problem can be formulated in specific terms that leads to task-centered intervention. It is important to note that this treatment approach is appropriate only in **reactive** emotional problems. If the emotional problem is not reactive, medical and psychiatric treatment is indicated and the social worker refers the client to other sources of help.

Unlike psychodynamic models of treatment, the task-centered approach does not involve a lengthy diagnostic appraisal. Diagnostic thinking is problem-oriented and consists of exploring, identifying and analyzing target problems. The caseworker's judgments are concerned mainly with "definitions and explanations of the problem rather than with the client's personality or situation in any comprehensive way" (Reid and Epstein, 1972, pp. 75–76). Task-centered casework is basically pragmatic in approach and focuses on developing actions that clients can undertake to resolve problems rather than giving attention to the psychodynamic aspects of the client's feelings or behavior.

Crisis Intervention

Crisis intervention is widely used to help clients cope with stressful life situations: the onset of a serious illness, the loss of a loved one, a drastic change in status or in living arrangements or a sudden alteration of social role. More than any other model of psychotherapy, crisis intervention is strongly interdisciplinary in theory and practice.

Crisis intervention theory begins with the concept of homeostatic balance—the need for the individual to maintain a reasonable balance between affective and cognitive functioning. A crisis is seen as a disruption of the individual's emotional balance brought about by a traumatic event.

Resolution of a Crisis. In attempting to resolve a crisis, individuals go through the following phases:

1. When confronted with a problem, individuals use coping mechanisms that they have relied on to resolve past difficulties. Some of these habitual responses are adaptive; others are maladaptive and are not useful in dealing with the current problem.

2. An emotional crisis develops when individuals find that their past methods of solving problems are unsuccessful. Unable to cope with a stressful situation, they experience severe anxiety and emotional discomfort. At this point, individuals resort to random behavior in an attempt to relieve their emotional distress or to master the anxiety-provoking situation.

3. If previously learned coping behaviors prove ineffective, the mental confusion and emotional imbalance which follows interferes with the individual's problem-solving capacity. At this point, people usually begin to seek the help of others in solving their problems.

4. If the individual receives help in defining the problem and in understanding the feelings that accompany the crisis, an adaptive resolution to the stressful situation is made possible. The underlying conflicts represented in the crisis can be examined and partially resolved; the individual can mobilize internal and external resources to make decisions and resolve the crisis. The client's emotional distress is diminished and pre-crisis functioning can be restored within a brief period of intervention.

5. If the individual does not seek or find help in dealing with the problem or cannot develop new coping mechanisms, the crisis is eventu-

ally defused, but the underlying difficulty that produced the crisis remains unresolved.

Types of Emotional Crisis

Baldwin (1978) has developed a system for classifying emotional crises into six basic types that fall along a continuum, beginning with crises that involve external stress to crises that involve internal conflicts or psychopathology.

Dispositional Crises arise from a problematic situation with which clients need help, and intervention involves classifying the situation and providing the services needed. Intervention is not directed toward a resolution of the emotional factors involved.

Anticipated Life Transition Crises include anticipation of changes in the client's life situation such as career change, widowhood or retirement. Intervention involves psychological support and anticipatory guidance to help clients cope with the problems that are likely to occur during and after the transitions have occurred.

Sudden Traumatic Stress Crises result from an external stress that is unexpected and emotionally overwhelming (death of a spouse or family member) during which the client is immobilized. Intervention is aimed at helping clients recover from the initial shock and express negative feelings that are a result of the traumatic event they have experienced.

Maturational Crises result from developmental problems that cause distress and involve issues such as dependency, power and self-identity. Intervention focuses on helping clients react to the present problem situation in a more adaptive manner while simultaneously helping them to understand the psychodynamic issues involved.

Crises Resulting from Psychopathology occur when unresolved and serious pre-existing psychopathology impairs the ability of clients to resolve problems. In these cases, intervention focuses on helping clients resolve the presented problem and is aimed at providing appropriate supportive measures without encouraging excessive dependence. Therapy is therefore limited in scope and is not directed toward the resolution of the client's deep-seated psychological problems. After the client has been helped to cope with the current crisis, additional services may be required to treat the problem on a more intensive basis over a longer period of time.

Psychiatric Emergency Crises result when the individual is incompetent and unable to assume responsibility for resolving a serious problem, presents symptoms of acute psychosis, or acting-out behavior patterns. Immediate medical and psychological intervention may be required when there are indications that the client's condition has life-threatening possibilities. The primary responsibility of the therapist involves a rapid and accurate assessment of the client's condition and determining the need for immediate psychiatric treatment.

Characteristics of Crisis Intervention

Although mental health professional workers vary in the application of crises intervention, certain basic principles underlie this approach. They include the following:

First, crisis intervention focuses on the client's present problem and the event that led to the need for help. Because crisis intervention is time-limited, making a full psychodiagnostic evaluation is not possible. Making a rapid assessment is essential to effective crisis intervention and requires an ability to sift relevant information from irrelevant information obtained from the client.

Second, crisis intervention is active and direct but not unnecessarily directive. If the worker adopts a passive or over nurturing posture, the client will tend to become overly dependent and not work actively to resolve the crisis. Therefore, the worker must quickly and directly engage the client in the helping process. In some instances, direct advice and suggestions from the worker is needed, especially if the crisis must be quickly resolved.

Third, the worker must be skilled in the use of a wide range of treatment methods. Workers who are familiar with different models of intervention can be especially helpful by using a particular approach that is most effective in a given situation. Flexibility is important to meet the needs of a given client and achieve a particular goal within a short period of time. As Kardener points out: "It is the responsibility of the therapist to fit the therapeutic message with the needs of a given patient, and his particular desired goal, and not the patient's responsibility to fit a unimodal therapist" (1975, p. 8).

Fourth, there must be a minimum delay in initiating intervention. Help should be offered as soon as possible in order to ensure a positive response from the client. Clinics or mental health facilities with waiting lists are not able to offer crisis intervention. Agencies that require a full diagnostic evaluation before treatment begins are also unable to use crisis intervention, because the delays involved prevent the prompt attention to the client's immediate problem.

Fifth, goals must be clearly defined and time limits are set to achieve the goals. Therefore, contracting is an important component in crisis intervention. The contract sets out the goals to be achieved and spells out what is expected from worker and client. Time limits not only motivate the client to increase his efforts to resolve the crisis but also impel the worker to focus clearly on the current problem and work toward a rapid resolution.

Sixth, restoring the client's ability to think about the problem in an objective way is essential. During an emotional crisis, the client's ability to think about a stressful situation becomes confused and tends to result in feelings of hopelessness and helplessness. Helping clients begin to think more rationally at the outset of intervention is especially helpful in overcoming these feelings as clients begin to see that they can be in control of their situation and work toward a constructive resolution of the anxiety-provoking crisis.

Seventh, the client learns to use new approaches to resolving future crisis situations. Although the main goal of crisis intervention is to facilitate the client's return to a pre-crisis level of functioning as rapidly as possible, there is a possibility that clients will also adopt more useful ways of coping with problems and use the crisis experience to resolve underlying conflicts that surfaced in the course of the crisis. As a consequence, clients expand their repertoire of available coping skills.

Steps in Crisis Intervention

Crisis intervention involves three distinguishable phases: (1) assessing the nature and extent of the crisis; (2) contracting with the client as to goals of intervention and setting time limits; and (3) outlining the strategy to be employed in resolving the crisis.

Assessing the Crisis. Several aspects of the precipitating event are studied in the assessment process. Helping the client define the time and place of the event that triggered the emotional crisis is essential to developing an understanding of how and when the emotionally hazardous event occurred. Harris, Kales and Freeman (1963) point out that the client does not always recognize the source of stress that resulted in an emotional crisis:

While the events evoking conflict are remembered by the patient, they may not be reported, at least immediately, and are often not specifically connected with subjective distress. To establish such connections is the primary task of the therapeutic transaction. (P. 467.)

Assessment also includes an analysis of the interpersonal aspects of a crisis, especially if the loss of an important person upon whom the client was dependent is involved. Other dimensions of assessment include loss of self-esteem, loss of role functioning or loss of nurturing. When clients experience significant losses and try to replace them through maladaptive coping responses, an emotional crisis ensues.

The client's emotional reaction to the precipitating event is also an important element of assessment and helps determine if emergency measures need to be taken in the best interest of the client. Many clients will be experiencing guilt, anger, anxiety or depression. The nature and extent of these feeling states will help in making judgments about the ability of the client to cope with stress.

Assessing Coping Responses. Assessing the coping methods that clients use to a stressful situation leads to a more complete understanding of an emotional crisis. In some instances, clients use maladaptive coping responses to avoid responsibility for solving the crisis or may want to obtain secondary gains such as nurturance, attention or control. Maladaptive responses, once defined, can be discussed with clients. If these mechanisms serve a purpose of which clients are not fully cognizant, they will interfere with resolving the crisis.

Assessing the client's coping responses also includes defining alternative adaptive coping mechanisms and helping clients accept them. Usually, clients are afraid to risk making new responses. If they cling to their familiar maladaptive coping mechanisms, the therapist can engage them in examining what is at stake if they attempt to make alternative responses and gain a clearer understanding of why clients resist change.

Assessing Pre-Crisis Functioning. Determining how clients functioned just before the crisis occurred serves as a baseline against which a successful resolution of the present crisis can be measured. To make such an evaluation requires a study of the client's usual range of responses in coping with stress. Some clients have a very limited range, e.g. to attack or withdraw. Others have developed neurotic or regressive coping mechanisms in coping with stress.

The client's emotional level of awareness is also an important aspect of assessing pre-crisis coping. For example, some will have little or no recognition of feelings of anger, even when warranted, and experience only feelings of depression. Some clients will have been extremely expressive, while others have been guarded in showing either positive or negative feelings. Clients also vary in regard to what situations bring about significant emotional reactions. Asking clients to identify situations that cause them great difficulty or specific times when they have overreacted emotionally will give clues as to their pre-crisis functioning and their level of vulnerability. The client's self-image is also an important clue to pre-crisis functioning and will give some insight into what they consider to be strengths or weaknesses and how their personal assets can be used in coping with the current crises.

Contracting In Crisis Intervention.

Intervention in crisis situations involves a contract that addresses three issues: (1) the specific goals of crisis resolution; (2) the time limits on therapy; and (3) the therapeutic strategy to be used to achieve the goals within a limited time.

The specific goals are set out in concrete terms that the client can understand and agree to attain during therapy. The goals should be limited in number and be defined in behavioral terms or tasks to be carried out.

The worker and client then agree upon the time frame for attaining the goals, usually with a limit of six or eight sessions. The client is informed that the time limits are to be held to and therapy will not continue beyond the point agreed upon in advance.

The worker informs the client as to what is involved in the intervention process. The method employed will take into account the client's special needs, strengths and weaknesses as well as the goals to be achieved. The skill of the worker in the use of a variety of approaches is also a consideration. A wide range of skills is advantageous in crisis intervention as Kardener (1975) points out:

> Short-term therapists must be reasonably conversant with a variety of treatment modalities or seek collaborative consultation. It is the responsibility of the therapist to fit the therapeutic message with the needs of a given patient, and his particular desired goal, and not the patient's responsibility to fit a unimodal therapist. (P. 8.)

Carrying Out the Contract. Once the contract has been negotiated, the work of carrying it out begins. Several priorities must be kept in mind throughout the course of intervention:

First, safeguards must be taken against defusing the intervention process. The worker may inadvertently slip into methods that are appropriate for long-term therapy but defeat the aims of crisis intervention by assuming a passive rather than an active role in the helping process. Excluding extraneous material that is not relevant to the present problem is essential for crisis intervention to succeed. Attention must be consistently focused on the issues that relate to the client's method of coping with the presented problem.

Second, clients may resist changes that are required in order to resolve the crisis. As pointed out earlier, many clients risk giving up familiar patterns of coping even if they are ineffective. The client's resistance must be worked through if the contract is to be maintained and the crisis resolved.

Third, the emphasis on active involvement of the client in developing problem-solving skills is essential. The worker must be aware that some clients will regard the insistence on developing new coping skills as threatening. As Levinson so aptly observes, "The wish to be trusted far outweighs the wish to be cured" in some cases (1977, p. 483). By helping clients overcome resistance to problem-solving behavior, the therapist also enables them to be less vulnerable to stress in the future.

Terminating the Contract. The last interview should be used to evaluate the client's progress toward achieving the goals set out in the contract. At this point, the client can become more clearly aware of how previous methods of coping with stress have been ineffective and will also have gone through the difficulty involved in learning new responses to crises. On the basis of this understanding, clients can be helped to integrate what they have learned and anticipate applying their new insights to similar situations in the future. The use of anticipatory guidance is effective in making such an integration more likely, as Burgess and Baldwin (1981) suggest:

> Anticipatory guidance as a crisis intervention technique does help to prevent future crises by reinforcing client mastery. Yet use of this intervention is often omitted. Clients respond to it well and find it very useful to conceptualize in advance adaptive responses to problem situations. When this intervention is used, adaptive responses are more likely to occur in the future. Similar problems are then reduced to the status of an emotionally hazardous situation for which coping skills are available in lieu of progression to an emotional crisis. (P. 63.)

Application of Crisis Intervention. Crisis intervention in working with older persons can be employed in a variety of counseling situations, especially those cases in which the loss of an important person or value is involved. The following case illustrates how it can be effective in helping an older person cope with the impending death of a spouse.

Mrs. Childs, a 68-year-old woman, was referred for counseling when she learned that her husband's illness was diagnosed as terminal cancer and that he had only three months to live. In the initial interview, Mrs. Childs was obviously anxious and depressed. As she began to pour out her feelings about her husband's illness and impending death, she explained that she refused to discuss her feelings to her husband when she visited him at the hospital. She tried to keep a "stiff upper lip" but confessed to the counselor that when she returned home, she broke into tears. She could not bring herself to cry in her husband's presence, but each time she returned to visit him she had great difficulty trying to appear cheerful. She agreed she needed further counseling.

The initial interview with the social worker brought to light how Mrs. Childs coped with similar, but less serious situations in the past. She confessed that if something displeased her on her job, she would pretend it didn't bother her. She also kept her worries hidden from her husband because "I didn't want to have him burdened with my problems, and he had enough to worry about."

However, her previous defenses of avoidance and denial were not working in this situation. She was not sure she could visit Charles even one more time without breaking into tears and had come to the conclusion that she would have to talk with him about her grief. She lacked the courage to take this step, because "I've always been the strong one when it comes to facing a problem." Yet, she also knew that keeping her feelings hidden had become an intolerable burden. As she talked about her love for Charles, Mrs. Childs broke into tears and apologized for "breaking down."

The worker began to turn Mrs. Childs' attention on what she might do to resolve the problem, since it seemed that she would not be able to continue to restrain her feelings when she visited Charles. The only alternative began to become clear to Mrs. Childs as she and the worker talked about the next steps she would take. The worker suggested that, with Mrs. Childs' permission, she would visit with Mr. Childs in order to become acquainted with him and learn more about how he was reacting to his illness and how it was affecting his relation to his wife. Mrs. Childs said she did not know if her husband really knew that he would not get well, but she suspected that he probably knew that he "couldn't pull through."

Before the next scheduled interview, the worker talked with Mr. Childs and found that he did know that he was not going to recover, but he had tried to keep this from his wife because "she just couldn't deal with it." The worker told Mr. Childs that perhaps he was underestimating his wife's ability to cope with the problem. Mr. Childs then began to tell the worker that he was trying to "be strong," but he would really like to share his feelings about his impending death with his wife. "I think she ought to know how much I love her, and I think we ought to go through this together. I guess I need her more than ever, now."

Mrs. Childs was much relieved when the worker told her about the conversation with Mr. Childs. "I guess we just haven't been able to talk about things even though we both wanted to. Now, I think we can." The worker encouraged Mrs. Childs to take the first steps to open up channels of communication and assured her that Mr. Childs would welcome a chance to talk with her honestly about his feelings now that he knew that he would not recover.

In the next interview, Mrs. Childs appeared much improved. Her previous anxiety and depression had greatly diminished. She expressed relief and gratitude because "Charles and I really feel closer to each other than we have for a long time. We needed to take the first step, and now we can go ahead and face things much better and together. We can share the pain, but we can also share our love."

As this case illustrates, identifying clients' feelings and anxieties is essential in the initial phase of crisis intervention, and identifying the coping mechanisms can also be accomplished early on in the helping process. In this case, the client's problem could not be resolved until she was able to give up her attempts to hide her true feelings and relate to her husband in a non-protective way. She also learned that she was not really helping Mr. Childs by keeping her grief from him and that he wanted to share feelings rather than repress them.

Evaluation of Crisis Intervention. Howard Parad was one of the first social work theoreticians to recognize the potential of crisis intervention as a useful approach in social work practice. He maintained that short-term intervention could be effective in mobilizing the client's untapped ego strengths to solve problems resulting from a stressful life situation. Lydia Rapoport (1970), one of the most articulate thinkers in crisis intervention, saw that this form of intervention required modification of traditional social work methods and pointed out that practitioners needed to develop skill in making an accurate assessment of the client and the client's life situation; that they must be able to work quickly toward restoring the client's functioning within a limited time frame.

As crisis intervention has become widely accepted as an effective approach in helping clients cope with stressful situations, it has been used in a variety of settings. The application of crisis intervention to working with older persons who are trying to cope with significant changes that accompany aging can be seen within the broad framework of what this model is designed to accomplish and how it relates to problems of the elderly.

First, the crisis intervention model gives equal attention to the internal and external factors that produce stress. This basic view is appropriate in assessing the problems of older persons because they are often called upon to deal with external, interpersonal and environmental factors at a time when their mental, physical and emotional resources have been depleted. Therefore, timely and effective intervention is badly needed to help them cope with stressful situations. Crisis intervention is designed to fill this need and can be effective in resolving concrete problems such as lack of financial resources to dealing with more complex psychological and emotional conflicts or difficulties that are common in older segments of the population.

Second, crisis intervention focuses on the presented problem as the change-target in the helping process. Since the coping capacities of older persons are usually at low ebb in time of crisis, a concentration on mobilizing the client's internal and external resources is an essential part of helping. Because providing external sources of support is often necessary in working with older persons, the approach should also include working with the client's family, supporting network and community resources.

In some cases, more prolonged supportive measures are needed to sustain older persons after the immediate crisis has been resolved or the emotional impact of a stressful situation has subsided. Therefore, the need for longer-term supportive casework should be taken into account when crisis intervention is terminated. Older persons often need a continuing relationship to the helping person when coping with the death of a spouse or making a transition in status or style of living. Therefore, this form of short-term intervention may have limited benefit to clients who are undergoing difficulty in adjusting to retirement, to widowhood or to prolonged and untreatable illnesses.

The crisis intervention approach can be especially useful in helping older persons cope with trauma associated with an unexpected loss. Since older persons experience extreme anxiety and depression in the aftermath of an unexpected loss, such as death of a spouse, immediate help is indicated to prevent serious personal disorganization or suicide. In this way, crisis intervention is an important preventive measure that helps older persons survive significant loss.

Crisis intervention can be effectively employed in helping older persons who live alone and need immediate help from community agencies when an emergency arises. Training protective personnel, such as police, in the basic techniques of crisis intervention can be a useful way to guarantee that those older persons who are socially isolated and vulnerable to stress can be assured of prompt attention and appropriate assistance in time of crisis. Community mental health centers also can develop crisis intervention programs, including outreach services, that can meet the needs of older persons who are facing overwhelming problems that they are not prepared to solve or those who are unable to function adequately because of emotional or mental deficits.

Because knowledge about the nature of emotional crises and skill in using the structure of crisis intervention are essential to a sound professional approach, social workers need to have adequate training in its use. Baldwin (1977) suggests that the following skills are essential in intervention practice.

First, setting time limits. Some clinicians have difficulty in setting explicit time limits with their clients and may fail to use the therapeutic value of a predetermined point for termination of intervention.

Second, workers need to become aware that specific and achievable goals are spelled out at the outset of contact with their clients. Expertise in setting goals to be achieved within a short time span is essential.

Third, maintaining a consistent focus on the present stress situation and resolving the client's current problem may also be difficult for workers who are inclined to explore other aspects of the client's situation and delay the helping process.

Fourth, workers need to become skilled at making a rapid assessment, screen out irrelevant information and formulate goals and strategies in a very brief period, usually in the first contact with the client.

Fifth, the crisis intervention requires the worker to adopt a more directly active role than in long-term therapy. At the same time, the temptation to become overcontrolling must be avoided.

Sixth, workers need to accept the limited goal of crisis intervention, i.e. to re-establish a level of adaptive functioning at the pre-crisis level in the shortest time possible.

Seventh, workers must develop skills in terminating intervention and be able to deal with the problems involved in separating from the client and ending the relationship after the presented problem has been resolved.

Eighth, the worker must be able to facilitate appropriate referrals after crisis intervention goals have been attained when clients require additional services. A comprehensive knowledge of community resources and an understanding of the mechanics of referral facilitate clients' efforts to obtain the help they need to which they are entitled.

The increased application of crisis intervention in a variety of settings will lead to a refinement of the process and result in a new, effective approach to helping older persons cope with stressful situations in a limited period of time and also enhance their capacity to deal with other similar problems in the future.

Summary

Crisis intervention and task-centered casework are similar in several important respects. Both are short-term in character and are designed to achieve specific objectives within a definite period. Both models are highly structured in their approach and set out a carefully constructed procedure to be followed in various stages of intervention. These two modes also bypass the traditional diagnostic process that focuses on psychodynamics and concentrate on a rapid appraisal of the problem that the client is trying to resolve. Because they are brief forms of treatment, they are both aimed at restoring the client's functioning as rapidly as possible and do not attempt to resolve underlying psychological problems in the client's personality structure.

The supportive casework approach is less structured than crisis-intervention and task-centered practice. The objectives of this mode of treatment are non-specific and more ambiguous in their formulation. Supportive casework is also open-ended in terms of duration of service and does not usually include a definitely stated contract between client and worker as a basis for intervention as is the case in task-centered and crisis intervention practice. The supportive casework model emphasizes the importance of the therapeutic relationship as a critical element in helping clients cope with problems, whereas crisis intervention and task-centered approaches place emphasis on structure and outcome as the primary consideration in the helping process.

In the chapter that follows, two methods of intervention that have developed out of social learning theory will be examined: behavior modification and cognitive therapy. The techniques employed in these two models can often be incorporated in social work practice to help older persons cope with emotional problems. The section on integrated counseling explores a comprehensive, eclectic form of social work intervention in working with the elderly.

Chapter 5

BEHAVIORAL, COGNITIVE AND INTEGRATIVE APPROACHES

Among the major approaches to helping older persons cope with emotional problems are: behavior modification, cognitive therapy and integrative social work intervention. In this chapter, each approach is described and evaluated.

Behavior Modification

Behavior modification can be briefly defined as an attempt to decrease maladaptive behavior and correspondingly increase adaptive behavior. The core of behavioral therapy consists of training clients to respond to specific situations in new ways so as to increase their behavior repertoire. Applied to older persons, it can be used to help them control anxiety and resolve emotional problems or disorders.

Characteristics of Behavior Therapy

The social learning model on which behavior therapy rests stands in contrast to traditional psychotherapy approaches that regard abnormal behavior as symptomatic of a more basic personality disturbance or underlying conflict. A behaviorist approach is based on the premise that emotional problems represent maladaptive behavior that has been learned and can be changed by specific techniques. Among the more important distinguishing characteristics of behavior therapy are these (O'Leary and Wilson, pp. 16–17):

1. Behavior modification views emotional problems as the way in which a person has learned to cope with stress and difficulties of living.
2. Abnormal behavior can be treated directly through the application of social learning principles rather than by "working through" presumed personality conflicts.

3. Behavior modification rejects psychoanalytic and personality trait labels to describe people and focus attention on what they think, feel and do in particular life situations.
4. Behavior modification entails an explicit specification of how treatment is to be conducted and a careful, objective evaluation of outcomes.

Applying the Behavioral Approach

The application of behavior modification involves a systematic evaluation of the presented problem based on direct observation of the client's behavior. For example, simply labeling the person as depressed is not a sound basis for intervention. Instead, the depression must be clearly stated in terms of observed behavior such as crying, refusal to eat, decline in sexual activity and withdrawal from social relations. Anxiety must be reduced to ways that the person behaves and the specific situations that precede and are associated with the behavior.

In contrast to traditional psychodynamic views, behavior therapy attempts to identify the environmental and self-imposed variables that currently maintain the individual's maladaptive behavior. Some maladaptive behavior is caused by "person variables," i.e. products of the individual's social learning that condition and affect his behavior. A depressed client may constantly "put himself down" and consider himself worthless even though it is clear to the objective onlooker that he is competent. In this case, therapy would be directed toward helping the individual correct faulty perceptions that are producing the depressive behavior. Another client may be depressed because he lacks the skills to achieve rewards that are important to him. In this instance, therapy would be directed toward helping the individual acquire the necessary skills and thereby overcome his behavioral deficit.

In making an assessment, the therapist explores the following areas: (a) the client's overt behavior; (b) affective responses such as anxiety or depression; (c) sensory reactions such as muscle tension; (d) emotive imagery, both positive and negative; (e) cognitive processes such as self-defeating verbalization; and (f) interpersonal relationships such as lack of assertion. The therapist next decides on a specific target behavior that is to be altered and the specific techniques that are to be employed to bring about such changes.

Systematic Desensitization. This technique is used to help older persons cope with situations that are anxiety-provoking and includes teaching them progressive relaxation exercises that will reduce anxiety by relieving muscle tension. Training in progressive relaxation involves a basic five-step process: (1) the individual is required to center attention on a specific muscle group (head, neck, arms, legs); (2) the individual is instructed to tense this muscle group for five or ten seconds and focus attention on the sensations that follow; (3) the individual is asked to relax the muscles; (4) the individual is required to focus attention on the sensations that occur after relaxation; and (5) the individual is instructed to maintain the relaxed state. The exercises are continued until the client has mastered the relaxation techniques. Training manuals and tape recordings can be used to practice relaxation exercises at home.

The purpose of desensitization is to develop new adaptive responses to situations that are anxiety-producing, using relaxation techniques in combination with imagery. The client is instructed to imagine a number of situations that create anxiety. Hierarchies of anxiety situations are constructed, ranging from mildly stressful to very threatening items. Clients are instructed to imagine these situations while they are deeply relaxed, beginning with the least-threatening situation and progressing to one that is severely anxiety-provoking. If a specific item produces excessive anxiety, clients may be instructed to repeat the exercise until they are able to visualize it without experiencing anxiety. Although the process is usually conducted imaginatively, real situations may be used to reduce the client's anxiety in specific situations.

For older persons, the technique can be employed in helping them cope with specific fears such as fear of being institutionalized, fear of being alone, fear of rejection or a dysfunction, either mental or physical. A study by Garrison (1978) showed that relaxation can be used to help older persons overcome anxiety by teaching them to understand the nature of anxiety, muscular relaxation training, and systematic desensitization. Elderly patients were required to complete a certain procedure: tension relaxation alternation, relaxation alone, differential and rapid relaxation, and imagining anxiety-producing scene while relaxed. Training lasted seven weeks and included homework.

Stress Inoculation Training developed by Meichenbaum (1973) is a procedure that helps clients manage anxiety through self-instructional training. This process involves three steps: (1) educating clients about the nature of anxiety; (2) asking clients to rehearse coping behaviors; and (3) practicing new skills in actual life situations. Clients are then asked to think of positive statements that would counteract their anxiety in a specific situation. These positive statements involve four areas: (1) preparation for the stressful event, (2) confronting the situation, (3) facing the possibility of being overwhelmed by the stressful situation, and (4) reinforcing the ability to succeed in coping with it.

Stress inoculation to control anxiety in elderly patients was employed by Hussian in working with four geriatric patients (mean age 79) who experienced extreme anxiety when imagining riding on an elevator. They resigned themselves to remain on their own floors at a long-term care facility and had given up hope of participating in outdoor activities. The residents were instructed to tell the therapist all the "outlandish things" that would happen if they entered an elevator: feeling of entrapment, being burned alive, being caught in the doors and plummeting four stories into the ground. After some discussion of these statements, the residents were asked to construct and repeat aloud positive statements such as "When the doors open, I will go inside and hold on to the rails," and "If the door sticks, I will not panic but push the red button until help arrives."

The residents were then instructed to imagine themselves approaching and entering an elevator while rehearsing the positive statements. At the end of five training sessions, all of them accompanied the therapist on a one-story ride. Two months later, all were riding the elevator several times a day and experienced no anxiety.

Self-instructional training can be used in a number of situations to help elderly persons make a successful adjustment to changes in their physical and mental functioning. Many older persons are prone to label themselves as inadequate and incompetent. They give up before completing or even attempting to perform a given task, and they become inactive and withdrawn as a result of their internalized, negative self-image. After they have been trained to substitute rational, positive self-statements that reinforce attempting and completing tasks, their self-confidence is restored, their withdrawn, depressed and inactive responses are diminished and they become actively involved in their environment.

Assertion Training is a relatively new approach in helping older people develop new behavior patterns and is based on the theory that extreme passivity or extreme aggressiveness can lead to anxiety or depression, while an assertive stance enhances self-esteem and self-confidence. This approach is especially useful in working with older persons who are often relegated to the sidelines or who allow themselves to be pushed aside too easily. Assertion training enables older persons to avoid being treated in a patronizing manner, as if they were not-too-bright children, being demeaned or treated with cold indifference. Some older persons fight back, but many accept an internalized image that makes them begin to think of themselves as totally inadequate and take on patterns of behavior that fit the stereotype of aging in our youth-oriented culture.

Assertive training is aimed at helping older people develop skills and does not carry the implication that an individual is sick or maladjusted. It is specifically designed to help people deal with day-to-day situations. Many older persons are unable to refuse unreasonable requests, do not stand up for their rights, and are often taken advantage of by more dominant people. Accordingly, their sense of self-esteem and personal dignity is greatly diminished and their anxiety about participating in social situations becomes a significant emotional problem. The objective of assertion training is to teach clients a new repertoire of appropriately assertive behavior and to help them distinguish between aggressive behavior, non-assertive behavior and assertive behavior.

Assertion training involves role-playing scenes in which individuals participate to act out new behavioral responses to certain situations which are anxiety-provoking and stressful. Because role playing is an essential element of assertion training, it is used with groups rather than individuals.

Behavior Rehearsal is another technique used to develop appropriate behavioral competence and social skills. This technique requires that clients engage in role playing and rehearsing assertive responses. The therapist models the appropriate assertive behavior and then asks clients to engage in a graduated sequence of similar actions until it becomes an acceptable form of response. Clients are then encouraged to practice assertive behavior by carrying out "homework" assignments. In role playing, the therapist focuses on developing non-verbal as well as verbal forms of expression, including body posture, voice training and eye contact. Assertion training through behavioral rehearsal is especially recommended in groups where unassertive older persons can practice new ways of responding and benefit from positive feedback from other group members. As Alexander and French (1946) observe, the ability to succeed in developing new, positive forms of behavior has great therapeutic value:

No insight, no emotional discharge, no recollection can be as reassuring as accomplishment in the actual life situation in which the individual failed. Thus, the ego regains that confidence that is the fundamental condition, the prerequisite of mental health. Every success encourages new trials and decreases inferiority feelings, resentments and their sequelae—fear, guilt and resulting inhibitions (P. 40).

Participant modeling and behavior rehearsal experiments indicate that it supports clients' efforts to cope with anxiety situations more effectively and that, in some instances, it is preferred to desensitization in the treatment of phobic disorders.

Depression and Behavior Therapy

Studies suggest three categories of depression that respond to behavior modification:

1. **Exaggerated and Prolonged Reaction to Loss.** If a grief reaction is sustained over an extended period, individuals often become depressed because the loss of an important person has not been replaced and they are unable to accommodate to the loss.
2. **Reactive Depression Associated with Anxiety.** A depression may result from a failure of the individual to resolve anxiety that is provoked by a stressful life situation. The individual becomes exhausted in the continual failure of efforts to cope with the stress and ultimately gives up trying to find a solution. A sense of helplessness and depression replace the original feeling of anxiety.
3. **Failure to Control Interpersonal Situations.** Depression may result when an individual feels dominated by another individual and is unable to deal with the issue of control by appropriate assertive behavior, as is often the case with older persons who become dependent and are conditioned to responding in submissive behavior patterns.

Several strategies are available to counteract depressive behavior. The worker may reinforce the client's positive relationship with persons in the environment to compensate for loss. Or the client may be encouraged to take the initiative in forming new relationships. Behavior rehearsal, assertion training or desensitization may be used to reduce anxiety and improve social skills.

Dengrove (1966) has used systematic desensitization in working with clients who are depressed because of the loss of a loved person and are experiencing prolonged grief reactions. The client is asked to recall the lost person in a variety of happy situations that occurred in the past. When the client has attained a state of deep muscle relaxation, he is asked to recall a series of such pleasant events in sequence leading up to the lost person's death and funeral. The client is then able to cope with anxiety associated with the loss and also experience relief from the depressive symptoms.

Social Work and Behavior Modification

There is little doubt that the techniques of behavior modification are effective in dealing with some specific emotional problems. Systematic desensitization can reduce anxiety. Assertion training can result in significant change in behavior, modify interpersonal relationships and develop social skills that clients often lack. The use of behavioral rehearsal and role modeling are also important techniques that can be employed in group therapy. In this regard, behavior modification has a legitimate place in social work with older persons.

Finally, traditional social work practice has grown out of psychodynamic theories that espouse extensive historical diagnosis and the use of psychiatric terminology in assessing emotional problems. This orientation has led to a focus on "talk therapy" that produces insight and greater self-awareness. Behavior modification therapists suggest there is little empirical evidence to support this contention:

> Much of what many consider to be "the" social work approach is a product of tradition and not of rational choice of a process through which social work goals can effectively be carried out. The choice of procedures to be employed by social workers to achieve their goals should be made on the basis of empirical evidence (i.e., what works) rather than on emotion (i.e., it's what I know; what I've always done; what our leaders say is right; or what I feel comfortable with). Neither tradition nor uncontrolled clinical impressions would seem the best criteria for the selection of an intervention system. What matters is, does it really help? (Fischer and Gochros, 1975, p. 480.)

Cognitive Therapy

Cognitive therapy is designed to alleviate or eliminate psychological distress by correcting faulty perceptions and irrational thought patterns that underlie depression, anxiety and other emotional or behavioral disorders. Cognitive therapy suggests that the individual's problems are derived from certain distortions of reality based on erroneous premises and assumptions. Therapy consists of helping a patient unravel his distortions in thinking and learn alternative, more realistic ways to formulate his experiences.

Base of Cognitive Therapy

The roll that faulty thinking plays in causing emotional problems has been explored by several psychotherapists. Among them is Albert Ellis, the founder and leading theorist of rational-emotive therapy, a well-defined form of cognitive therapy. The basic premise of rational-emotive therapy can be briefly stated as follows: emotional reactions, such as depression, are not caused by events but are the result of how these events are interpreted and evaluated. Therefore, helping people cope with emotional problems involves questioning, challenging and disputing the irrational belief that causes them to become depressed, fearful or hopeless. The purpose of this process is to enable people to recognize that their beliefs are absurd, to relinquish them and adopt new ways of thinking and responding to emotionally disturbing situations and events.

The practice of cognitive therapy rests on the following principles:

1. **Mood States Depend on Cognition.** How people feel depends on what they believe or tell themselves. If they tell themselves that events are catastrophic, they will feel hopeless and depressed. If they expect that they will be unable to cope with a given event, such as a decline in their health, they will in fact become helpless.
2. **Imaging and Fantasy Contribute to How People React to Given Situations and Have Enormous Influence Over People's Emotions and Behavior.** When they are asked to imagine something frightening (making a public speech), they react as though the event were actually taking place. Using imagination has proven to be a valuable tool in helping people deal with emotional problems by desensitizing them to an anxiety-provoking event or situations.
3. **Cognition, Emotion and Behavior are Interrelated.** Cognition contributes to emotion and action; emotions also contribute to cognition. Experiments show that when people change their behavior, they also begin to think and feel differently. Changing ways of thinking also changes feelings and behavior. Effective therapy therefore teaches people a variety of techniques they can use in changing their thinking, their emotional responses and their behavior. Clients

in cognitive therapy need to see the complex reasons for their emotional disturbance; how they will have to work to avoid falling back to dysfunctional behavior that they have previously overcome.
4. **Expectations Influence Behavior.** What people expect to happen or how they expect others to act has an important effect on how they themselves behave. Cognitive behavior therapy uses clients' expectations to help them overcome their emotional disturbances.
5. **Attribution Errors Influence Emotions and Behavior.** People attribute motives, reasons and causes to other people or events. A good deal of their emotional disturbance is caused by false perception, and cognitive therapy is directed toward helping people understand and change them.

Cognitive Approach to Depression

Cognitive therapy has been useful in treating reactive depression in later life. Beck has developed a systematic approach to cognitive therapy based on the premise that there are five logical errors that cause people to become depressed: arbitrary inference, selective inference, overgeneralization, magnification, and personalization.

Arbitrary inference refers to drawing conclusions for which there is no evidence. Selective inference refers to drawing conclusions based on some particular fact or detail taken out of context. Magnification refers to reaching conclusions that assume the worst possible consequences of a certain course of action. Personalization refers to linking some particular event to oneself when there is no basis for making such a connection.

Beck and others have developed two steps in using this technique to treat depression: (1) the therapist examines the life history of the patient to uncover and demonstrate that depressive thoughts and beliefs were learned in the past; and (2) patients are taught to uncover statements and thoughts that are depressing and examine them objectively.

The depressed person regards himself as a loser. He believes he has lost some important and irreplaceable value such as a personal relationship or that he has failed to achieve some significant goal in life. Moreover, the depressed individual expects that any action he takes will end in failure; therefore, he will avoid engaging in any constructive activity. In addition, he feels that he is inferior, inept and lacks self-worth. These negative concepts produce the symptoms of depression: sadness, passivity, self-blame, loss of pleasure responses and suicidal thoughts.

To alter these symptoms, the cognitive therapist helps the patient examine the assumptions that underlie the depression and test the hypothesis on which his thinking is based. By questioning, the therapist engages the patient in a debate that forces a confrontation as to what is rational and what is irrational and opens the patient's "closed system" of thinking to new information and a reevaluation of his self-image.

To reinforce changes in thinking, the therapist tests the patient's view of personal inadequacy by assigning activities that will provide tangible evidence for changes in his usual thinking pattern. The therapist starts by assigning a simple task that is well within the patient's capability. As the patient experiences success in carrying out the task, his perception of his capacities changes and he can begin to see himself as competent rather than inadequate. Homework assignments are given at each session and the patient is expected to carry out specific activities that will counteract the depression.

Several positive results from this activity are: (1) the patient sees himself as more masterful; (2) he becomes more optimistic as his self-esteem increases; (3) the activity distracts him from his usual depressing thoughts; (4) other people begin to see him in a more positive light and reinforce his self-image as a competent person; and (5) the patient begins to enjoy activity and receives pleasure from engaging in the assigned tasks.

To motivate the patient to engage in activity, the therapist questions his reasons for not wanting to undertake the assigned task. Most depressed patients have developed avoidance systems that prevent them from acting in a constructive way. Reasons given by patients include such statements as: "I'm too tired or weak." "It is pointless to try." "I will fail at anything I try." The therapist exposes these locked-in self-defeating attitudes and asks the patient to examine them critically. The goal is to train the patient to identify these negative thoughts and be able to challenge them spontaneously without help from the therapist.

Application of Cognitive Therapy

In view of the fact that older persons do experience losses of health, loss of status or loss of a significant person, a cognitive approach can be useful in helping the elderly cope with such losses with less emotional trauma. In short, older persons can learn to gain "cognitive mastery" by analyzing the irrational thoughts and meanings that result from traumatic events. As Beck (1976) has noted, "The thesis that the special meaning of an event determines the emotional response forms the core of the cognitive model of emotions and emotional disorders. This meaning is encapsuled in a cognition—a thought or an image" (p. 52).

The "primary triad in depression" as described by Beck has special relevance to the emotional problems of older persons. The first component is the pattern of construing experiences in a negative way. Depressed persons selectively or inappropriately interpret events. They feel thwarted or defeated, interpret trivial events as a substantial loss or interpret neutral remarks as ridicule and disparagement. The second component is a negative view of self and is associated with self-rejection. Clients who are depressed see themselves as inferior and castigate themselves for being inferior. They also have negative expectations. When they contemplate undertaking a task, they predict they will fail. They view the future in a negative way and anticipate that current difficulties or suffering will continue indefinitely. These negative views of self, the world and the future result in paralysis of the will, escapist and avoidance wishes, suicidal wishes and intensified dependency wishes.

Older persons are especially prone to develop these negative views, tend to become apathetic and withdraw from activity. They lose motivation to attempt any course of action because they expect a negative outcome and are stripped of internal stimulation to do anything. The techniques of cognitive therapy are designed to overcome the "primary triad" that results in depressive symptoms and dysfunctional behavior associated with aging. For example, "success therapy" in which clients are assigned to carry out graded tasks that can be accomplished counteracts the negative self-image. Another technique that is helpful in dealing with depression and feelings of incompetence is mastery and pleasure therapy (Beck, 1976) in which the client keeps a daily record of activities and marks down an "M" for every activity that provided a sense of mastery and "P" for every activity that provided some pleasure.

Two additional techniques are useful in helping older persons overcome the negative triad. One is the identification of automatic thoughts that create emotions such as sadness or that result in negative behavior. Clients are asked to keep a daily record of their dysfunctional automatic thoughts, write a rational response to them, and rate the degree to which they believe the rational response. Another technique is cognitive rehearsal in which clients imagine going through the steps of some anxiety-provoking situation and report anticipated difficulties and obstacles they will encounter. These homework exercises pinpoint the automatic thoughts that prevent positive response and effective action. Once identified, clients can begin to deal with negative thoughts in a rational way.

Problem Solving and Cognitive Therapy

Older people differ greatly in how well they handle problem situations. When they are unable to cope with problems, they become anxious or depressed because they cannot act effectively. A problem-solving approach helps older persons to make effective responses to problem situations and reach decisions based on rational considerations.

Problem solving is a cognitive approach to therapy based on the assumption that ineffectiveness in coping with problems results in emotional or behavioral disorders and that training individuals in problem-solving skills enables them to deal with the challenges of day-to-day living. The main objective in the problem-solving approach is to identify a problem and to develop the client's ability to choose an effective solution to the presented difficulty. The process results in establishing a sense of competence and self-reliance that is essential to a high morale and emotional stability.

Training individuals to become effective in problem solving involves five stages: (1) general orientation, (2) problem definition and formulation, (3) generating alternative solutions, (4) decision making, and (5) verification.

General Orientation. The purpose of general orientation in the early phase of problem solving is designed to help clients realize that problems are a normal part of life and that it is important to recognize problems as they occur. Clients are also taught that they can cope with problems and will be able to find adequate solutions even if no immediate course of action seems possible. Dollard and Miller (1950) maintain that if a person responds immediately when confronted with a problem, there may not be sufficient time to reach a rational, effective solution. Clients are therefore taught to avoid hasty, impulsive decision making.

Problem Definition and Formulation. At the outset, most problems in living are ambiguous and lack necessary facts and information. Defining all aspects of a situation in concrete terms and formulating of classifying the problem appropriately is an essential step in problem solving. Defining a problem forces the client to consider all aspects of a situation and make certain that all relevant facts are taken into account. The problem can then be analyzed more carefully to determine what issues are involved. For example, a problem may be formulated as having to choose between two conflicting goals or it may be formulated as an obstacle that needs to be dealt with in trying to attain a goal.

Generating Alternative Solutions. This is the core of problem solving and involves the development of a wide range of possible responses to the problem situation. Alternative solutions must be stated in operational terms. They may represent "strategies" or "tactics." Strategies are more general in character and indicate **what** to do in a given situation. Tactics are more specific and indicate **how** to carry out a given solution. In the beginning stage of generating alternatives, clients will concentrate on developing different strategies that could be pursued rather than choosing tactics.

Decision Making. Once alternative strategies have been developed, clients must decide which are worth pursuing and which alternatives will be most useful in achieving specific goals. Clients are asked to review each possibility and ask: "If I were successful in carrying out this particular course of action, what would be the likely consequences?" Although not all possible consequences can be predicted, clients can guess what is most likely to occur and use their best judgment to determine whether the consequences would be desirable or undesirable. Some problems are not amenable to a really "good" solution, and in such cases, choices are made on a relative, rather than an absolute, basis.

Verification. Up to this point, clients have been thinking rather than doing. Problem solving is not completed until the client takes a course of action and then verifies how effective the action has been. Verification involves observing the consequences of one's own actions. If the client is satisfied with the consequences, the problem-solving process can be ended. Should the solution not come up to the client's expectations, the client must resume the process to arrive at a better alternative. In some cases, clients may not be able to carry out the best alternative course of action or be too anxious about behaving in certain ways. A careful assessment of the client's inhibitions and capabilities can determine if additional treatment such as desensitization, rational restructuring or behavior rehearsal is indicated.

Application of Problem Solving. Many so-called dependent clients who cannot cope with problem situations on their own can benefit from this approach. Some older persons have adequate performance skills but are not able to put them to use because they lack problem-solving ability.

In such cases, the goal is to teach them new problem-solving skills and avoid providing solutions for them. Some clients have good problem-solving skills but are lacking the ability to carry out solutions because of emotional inhibitions. They can be helped by assigning graded tasks to overcome their anxiety. In such cases, problem solving would need to be combined with behavior rehearsal or systematic desensitization.

Problem solving can be beneficial when clients are going through a transition in role status and will need to adjust to changes in their environment or life-style. Women who become widows are often in need of help in coping with problems after the death of their husbands and can benefit from a problem-solving approach that makes them more competent in dealing with day-to-day problems. Older persons who are faced with having to make important changes such as moving into a long-term care facility can also be helped to arrive at a satisfactory alternative solution through problem solving. Many older persons also need help in carrying out solutions and can benefit from therapy that will make it possible for them to respond in new and more effective ways when problems occur.

In general, problem solving can be applied in a broad spectrum of situations to help clients become more independent as they acquire problem-solving skills. Toward the end of therapy, clients must come to realize that they must rely on their own resources and skills without the direct advice and direction of the therapist. Although this may be difficult for them, the ultimate goal is to develop their competence in problem solving and increase their feelings of adequacy and self-worth.

Integrative Counseling

Integrative counseling, an eclectic approach especially designed for work with older persons, is an outgrowth of the work of Edmund Sherman at the School of Social Welfare of the University of New York at Albany and the Albany Center for Psychotherapy. The essential characteristics of this approach have been summarized by Sherman (1981):

> The central focus of the approach is to identify, use and enhance the normal development of personality functioning in the later years of adulthood as the basis for counseling older persons. The underlying theme of the approach is that certain capacities and strengths are normally developed in the course of aging which enable older persons to overcome the demoralization attendant upon the losses and prob-

lems of aging. When these capacities have not become operative because of circumstances or events, they should be uncovered, strengthened and developed in the counseling process (P. 27).

Treatment Continuum in Counseling

The integrative model of intervention suggests a continuum of treatment as a guide for the selection of goals in different types of problems or situations. Tasks that are appropriate in working with aging persons include: (a) providing maintenance conditions and services, (b) providing support and coping strategies, (c) encouraging internal locus of control, and (d) evolving alternate self-evaluations.

Providing Maintenance Conditions and Services. The integrative model recognizes that material needs and services have great importance in the lives of older persons and that material needs must be met before attempting to deal with the client's emotional problems. The objective is to reduce the stress caused by lack of material resources. During this phase, the worker seeks out the appropriate sources of help, makes referrals to community agencies that can supply the needed services and follow through to see that clients actually receive the assistance to which they are entitled. The approach in this phase is largely supportive and directive.

Providing Support and Coping Strategies. This stage in integrative counseling calls for supporting clients and assisting them in developing effective coping strategies. This phase is focused on psychological aspects of the client's situation and is designed to stabilize the individual's self-esteem, sustain morale and coping efforts. The objective is to improve social functioning but does not involve significant changes in behavioral, emotional or cognitive functioning.

Encouraging Internal Locus of Control. This phase of counseling calls for the worker to bring about better internal control, making clients feel that they are in charge of their life situation. To this end, counseling focuses on enhancing clients' problem-solving and coping skills. Behavioral techniques are used to help clients achieve "cognitive mastery" in solving problems.

Evolving Alternate Self-Evaluations. This phase is designed to bring about positive changes in self-concept, improve self-esteem and enable clients to evaluate themselves in alternative ways. Society generally uses a functionalistic standard as the basis for judging an individual's worth. The functionalistic value standard places great emphasis on productivity or monetary values. This ethical system denegrates the worth of an old person's role in a highly competitive, materialistic economy. In contrast, the integrative approach places great importance on the value of persons in their own right. Clients are helped to accept this principle of self-worth and believe in their value regardless of their previous history or their socio-economic status. As an alternative to the functionalistic ethic, this is an appropriate basis for self-evaluation by those older persons who are retired and whose physical decrement precludes participation in the work force.

Components of Integrative Counseling

The major components of integrative counseling consist of (1) the self component, (2) the locus-of-control component, (3) the value component, and (4) the morale component.

The self component includes the way in which individuals perceive themselves. It involves an image of the ideal self and the real self. Individuals struggle to achieve an ideal self, but they are rarely able to do so. If there is a wide discrepancy between the ideal self and the real self, feelings of failing and inadequacy occur. The self is also responsible for organizing and evaluating stimulus from the environment, i.e. there is a cognitive function that the self carries out in thinking and making judgments. How events are perceived depends on the cognitive self's appraisal and interpretation of the event.

The locus of control is an important aspect of aging and refers to the degree to which older persons feel they have control over events. Older persons tend to see themselves as either powerful or powerless. Those who perceive themselves as being in control of their life situation are more apt to adapt to stressful situations, are more inclined to take steps to help themselves, and respond more enthusiastically to therapy. In contrast, those who are prone to see control as outside themselves are waiting for the therapist to perform a miracle that will solve all their problems. To obtain the goals of integrative therapy, clients need to be encouraged to develop an internal locus of control.

Value clarification is an important component of integrative counseling, because self-evaluation is based upon the individual's own value system. Clients who hold on to a functionalistic system of values will often present symptoms of emotional distress that are associated with loss of status, a sense of failure and dissatisfaction with self and low self-esteem.

Integrative counseling regards morale or life satisfaction as the end product of intervention. This concept grows out of Erikson's view of integrity as the desired state in older adult life. As Sherman suggests, "In most cases we explicitly intend that clients should feel better about themselves as well as about their life circumstances, and in many cases our goal is a greater general life satisfaction that is not restricted to present circumstances. Ultimately, of course, we would hope that our clients could achieve a state of ego integrity that would of necessity include a good deal of life satisfaction and relatively high morale" (p.88).

Assessment Procedures and Instruments

In short-term counseling, an extensive assessment is not needed, but in more extended intervention various instruments are used to measure the clients' morale, their views of themselves and others, and the attitudes that have relevance at this stage in life.

Morale is measured by a Life Satisfaction Index that contains twenty statements. A positive response to a statement is scored as 1 and a negative or doubtful response receives a zero. Clients are required to agree or disagree with each statement. For example, an "agree" response to the statement, "As I grow older, things seem better than I thought they would be," is scored as a positive response and indicates a high level of life satisfaction. The score on this test is used as a base for judgments about morale and also serves to measure progress or regression during the course of counseling (Sherman, 1981, p. 240).

The Subjective Units of Disturbance Scale is used to determine the extent to which a given situation is anxiety-provoking on a scale of zero (absolute calm) to 100 (absolute panic). Clients are asked to rate their anxiety on this scale as their own subjective perception of their discomfort level. For example, if high anxiety is associated with driving a car, the client would score this in the upper end of the scale. The score indicates how well the client is coping with real or imagined life situations.

The Beck Depression Inventory provides a rapid assessment of the severity of a depression and also indicates if clients view themselves as failures or incompetent persons who can accomplish little without help from others. The inventory identifies the areas in which the client is experiencing the greatest discomfort and pinpoints target symptoms in the early phase of counseling.

The Cognitive Mastery Assessment Questionnaire is used to measure the degree to which clients feel that they are in control of their lives. The questionnaire consists of three simple and clear statements to which the client may respond by "strongly agree," "agree," "disagree," or "strongly disagree" (Sherman, 1981, p. 242).

The Functionalistic Ethic Assessment Questionnaire is an attempt to operationalize the client's reaction to four statements that indicate the degree to which clients hold to the functionalistic view of self-worth. For example, clients are asked to respond on a scale of "strongly agree" to "strongly disagree" to the following statement: "Unless I feel that I have accomplished or done something that other people value, I feel quite worthless" (Sherman, 1981, p. 243).

The Semantic Differential Test attempts to measure the discrepancy between the clients' ideal self and actual self. Improvement in the client's attitude toward self is indicated when the actual self is seen as not far removed from the ideal self. These evaluations are made by clients' own judgments as to strong, positive assets and negative, weak qualities about themselves and important others. Less discrepancy between the "ideal me" and the "me" indicates increased self-esteem (Sherman, 1981, p. 74).

Theoretical Base of Integrative Counseling

The integrative approach to the emotional problems of aging does not rest on one basic theoretical frame of reference. Indeed, the very term **integrative** suggests that the model attempts to borrow useful knowledge and concepts from several sources and integrate the views of various schools of psychotherapy into a comprehensive form of intervention.

The developmental view of aging as first formulated by Erikson in the eight stages of life has been incorporated in integrative practice, particularly in regard to the crucial task of reconciling despair and ego-integrity in the end of life. The emphasis on values and morale as prime issues in working with older persons reflects a concern about the quality of life of elderly people and the need to help them avoid feelings of uselessness and hopelessness that result in despair. Sherman suggests that in an important sense, the "integrative approach is a psychophilosophy, and the key to the whole approach is compassionate acceptance of self—past, present and future" (p. 238).

The social reconstruction model developed by social psychologist Bengston has also been incorporated in the integrative model, with some important modifications. The ideas of social breakdown as a source of difficulty among aged persons is basic to this view of social gerontology and is basic to the integrative model's emphasis on what Bengston refers to as "a benign cycle of competence through social systems input." To restore competence, older persons need inputs that build up coping skills, that reduce dependence and increase self-reliance, that result in older persons seeing themselves as effective. The inputs that are necessary to accomplish these ends include: (a) liberation from the functionalistic value system; (b) improved maintenance conditions such as housing, health, nutrition and transportation; and (c) encouragement of internal locus of control and building problem-solving skills (Bengston, 1973). This model of social reconstruction has been incorporated in the four objectives of the integrative counseling approach and the treatment continuum outlined by Sherman with the addition of morale as an important component of counseling.

Life review and reminiscence are included in integrative counseling as useful tools to help older persons make rational judgments about self-worth. Reminiscence can enable clients to identify with past achievements and positive events to enhance self-esteem and fortify their self-concept. Life review is also used to dispute retrospective generalization—the negative distortion of past events that is often the cause of despair. In many instances, clients hold themselves responsible for events over which they had little or no control and are overwhelmed by intense guilt and self-denigration. A technique for dealing with remorse and guilt is "disattribution" which involves teaching clients to stop blaming themselves by recognizing that fate, and the actions of others play an important role in such events. Self-blame can also be modified by using the cognitive restructuring technique, the ABC disputation model described by Ellis.

Another cognitive technique used in the integrative approach is distancing, a process in which clients are taught to view events objectively and attribute less blame to themselves as they begin to realize that they are only part of a complex set of circumstances that determine outcomes. Through distancing, clients are able to separate themselves from external events and reduce the impact they might have on their emotional state.

Alternative disputation is regarded as an essential in helping older persons cope with loss of role and self-esteem. This technique involves the presentation of arguments against the functionalistic ethics and is aimed at enabling clients to overcome the tendency to evaluate themselves only in terms of their performance. Older persons who have always given high priority to instrumental values as a measure of self-worth have great difficulty accepting a different standard by which to judge themselves. However, instrumental values assume less importance in the later years and can be replaced by alternatives that are essentially humane and compassionate in making self-evaluations.

Summary

A review of the behavioral, cognitive and integrative approaches to intervention indicates that there are some similarities and some distinguishable differences in their theoretical orientation and treatment techniques.

Behavior modification is based on the premise that emotional problems are conditioned or learned responses that can be altered by reconditioning techniques. Cognitive therapy agrees that emotional dysfunctioning is the result of conditioned responses to certain situations, but sees irrational thought patterns as the primary cause of depression and anxiety. The integrative model is based on a broad view of human development and incorporates supportive casework measures and cognitive therapy in working with older persons who present emotional problems.

All three models provide a framework for problem solving as a valid approach in intervention. Behavior modification is geared to solving specific problems such as non-assertive behavior or anxiety reactions. Cognitive behavior also addresses specific emotional problems, especially depression, and indicates how changes in thinking and perception can alleviate or eliminate specific emotional dysfunctions. The integrative approach gives major attention to correcting the self-defeating attitudes that are common among older persons using the techniques of cognitive therapy.

The problem-solving model provides a structured approach to intervention that is designed to assist clients in developing skills that can be transferred to a wide range of situations. The integrative model includes developing problem-solving capacity as an important objective in working with older persons and regards this capacity as essential to achieve a sense of internal control. In some respects, the problem-solving model is very similar to the task-centered casework approach. Both set forth a systematic structure for identifying target problems and developing alternative courses of action for the resolution of problems.

Sherman's integrative model is especially useful in working with older persons because it is based on an understanding of the psychodynamics of emotional problems that occur in late life and sets out the affective as well as the cognitive aspects of dysfunctions that are found among elderly persons. The emphasis on evolving alternatives in self-evaluation to reduce the impact of negative self-images is an important contribution to the understanding of how aging affects morale and how life satisfaction and feelings of ego integrity can be achieved. Sherman makes an interesting and insightful observation about what can be learned from those who attain ego integrity in old age.

> The lesson to be learned from the aged with ego integrity is that the adversity and losses they have sustained have served to move them toward a more mellow and compassionate view of themselves and others. It is not that they have benefitted from the pain of the losses they have suffered, but that they have learned that they cannot have what they cherish in a possessive sense, not even their egocentric self. The ultimate goal, then, is essentially acceptance—acceptance of life as a process, rather than as a possession, in a larger scheme of things. However, self-acceptance comes before acceptance of one's life, and this is the underlying theme of the integrative approach. (P. 239.)

Chapter 6

FAMILY THERAPY AND MARRIAGE COUNSELING

Several non-traditional approaches to helping older persons cope with emotional problems have recently emerged. Among these newer methods of intervention are family therapy, marriage counseling and sex therapy. Each of these methods serves a special purpose. Family therapy is designed to include adult children in solving the emotional problems of an aged parent by seeing the family members together as a group. The therapist helps the family arrive at solutions to the parent's problems through an exchange of ideas and clarification of feeling. Marriage counseling focuses on marital difficulties that often accompany changes in role and interpersonal relationships that affect the marriage. Counseling enables the couple to recognize that accommodations must be made if the relationship is to be sustained. Sex therapy is a more specialized form of therapy designed to deal with specific problems of sexual adjustment or sexual dysfunctioning.

Family Therapy

An increase in life expectancy indicates that many adult children will be involved in the care of an aging parent who is undergoing physical, mental or emotional stress or who can no longer live independently. Helping families cope with these problems is a matter of concern for mental health professionals in working with elderly persons. Most elderly people turn to family members, especially their adult children, for emotional support when they are experiencing losses, suffering from a chronic illness or becoming emotionally disturbed. Family therapy may be an effective way to help those who are most intimately involved in the life of an older client by offering group counseling to discuss problems that need to be resolved.

There is no one way to practice family therapy. Several different models have been developed, and although each approach has some distinguishing features, they all share the overall goal of strengthening the family unit. Some therapists are strongly influenced by psychoanalytic theory; some are grounded in communication theory. Virginia Satir's (1954) work in conjoint family therapy demonstrates the importance of teaching family members to communicate effectively. Jay Haley (1976) developed a problem-solving model that involves a structured sequence of stages, beginning with a specific problem that the family currently faces, defining the problem in terms of how family members contribute to the problem and requiring the family to take a course of action to resolve the difficulty. Haley prefers using a brief, intensive form of intervention rather than long-term therapeutic involvement. John Bell (1961), one of the first to experiment with family therapy, developed "family group therapy" as a problem-solving approach during which the family operates as a team in conference, working out more satisfactory ways of dealing with unsatisfactory relationships among family members. By working together to achieve certain goals, families attain a sense of unity that will enable them to maintain the changes that have taken place in the course of therapy.

Family therapy has been used in working with the elderly by John Herr and John Weakland at the Family Interaction Center of the Mental Research Institute in Palo Alto, California. Their work in "family centered applied gerontology" addresses problems of special concern to older persons: independence and loneliness, intergenerational struggles, alternative living arrangements, confusion, hypochondriasis, death, grief and grave disabilities. Herr and Weakland point out that the family centered approach is geared to achieving limited goals. Rather than looking toward long-term personality change, efforts are directed toward elders and their families solve situational problems. Intervention is not aimed at treating a specific psychological disorder but is limited to helping clients deal more effectively with the consequences of psychopathology. As Herr and Weakland (1979) point out, counseling elders and their families meets a special need.

> Being willing to counsel clients on situational problems is predicated on the belief that some relief from problems is better than no relief at all. While almost everyone would agree that it is ideally best to solve problems at the root cause, gerontological counselors ordinarily are unlikely to have the resources, time and expertise required for long-term psychotherapy aimed at fundamental personality change. However, it is a frequent observation among highly-trained psychotherapists that when dealing with emotional problems, success often breeds success.

Consequently, although you are not approaching the problems of your clients from a psychodynamic point of view, you may often note that clients who find their lives changing for the better are able to break the vicious cycle of defeatism so they can continue on an upward spiral toward making their lives better in other respects (P. 7).

The use of family therapy in working with older persons has gone more slowly than working with problems of children and young adults. But the work of Herr and Weakland suggests that the principles and techniques of a family centered approach can be successfully applied to help elders and their families solve a wide range of situational problems that are associated with aging.

Application of Family Therapy

When a slow deterioration or sudden crisis disables a parent, brothers and sisters are thrown together in an effort to solve the problems of an aged father or mother. A crisis may either bring adult children closer together or lead to intense rivalry and conflict. Sons may compete to gain exclusive claim over the father or mother's well-being and jockey to gain favor in the eyes of the parents. A child who feels that he or she has been in a less favorable position in the family may become overly solicitous to prove that they are worthy of parental love. Jealousy and rivalry among the siblings is reactivated and the family history repeats itself.

The Problem of Caretaking. As family members struggle to aid their parents, a crucial question arises: "Who is in charge?" Because daughters are considered to be closer to parents than are sons, they are more likely to be expected to take on major responsibility. A son may realize that he is in the best position to help. A daughter may volunteer to be the caretaker even though she has other family responsibilities. In some families, it is obvious that the parents prefer one particular child as caretaker, although they have not voiced a preference. One of the adult children may take responsibility because they live close by their elderly parents or have less family obligations. A favorite child may ask to be given this responsibility because he or she feels guilty about receiving more than the other children and wants to prove that he or she is worthy of this special position in the family.

The caretaker role can be a difficult one. The adult child who is in charge may be hated instead of loved by the rest of the family, or come under fire from brothers and sisters who charge that wrong decisions were made and who are quick to criticize while taking little or no responsibility for their aged parents. Caretakers sometimes become martyrs. Parents can be unreasonable in their demands and overburden the son or daughter who is responsible for meeting their needs. Caretakers may place unreasonable demands on themselves and become overzealous in carrying out tasks that other family members are unwilling to share. If the one child who is in charge does not ask for, or rejects, help when it is offered, he or she ends up with taking all responsibility and becomes the family martyr.

Family therapy sessions that include the adult children and their parents can be beneficial in helping the family reach a decision as to who is to take primary responsibility for the aged parents. Parents themselves may express their preference or determine what areas of their lives are not to be controlled by their children. These family sessions can prevent adult children from inflicting serious wounds on one another and their parents. Once family members are torn apart by disputes and conflicts, a cooperative effort to help their parents becomes highly improbable. Family therapy sessions can resolve many of these conflicts and be a valuable prevention and constructive step for aged parents and their children to undertake. At best, the outcome would develop a strong bond among family members. If not, at least bitter and unresolved acrimony may be avoided in the interest of the aged parents.

Resolving Feelings. When parents become dependent, their children will be called upon to deal with some negative and uncomfortable feelings that begin to surface when they watch a father or mother grow old. The most common feelings are fear and anxiety, anger and hostility, shame and guilt.

Adult children may never have developed a sense of independence and fear that once the protection of a strong father or a loving mother is gone, they will not be able to survive on their own. When they see that their parents are not healthy, vigorous persons, they become anxious. Parents sometimes reinforce such old patterns of dependence and even try to control their children's lives from their deathbeds. Illness and dependency can also reactivate strong feelings of anger in a child who has not had a happy relation to the aging father or mother, and recalls that his parents were thoughtless, punitive and derogatory throughout his or her childhood. Feelings of resentment solidify into a consistent pattern of hostility that is difficult to overcome. As Oscar Wilde wrote in *Dorian Grey,* "Children begin by loving their parents; as they grow older, they like them; later they judge them; sometimes they forgive them." Feelings of shame and guilt grow out of a wide range of issues and are experienced by most adult children when their parents grow old. They are ashamed of not having done enough, neglected to visit their parents or failing to provide financial support. Unfortunately, these painful emotions persist long after their parents have died.

Family therapy helps adult children deal with these disturbing feelings. Family members are encouraged to communicate their feelings openly and honestly in order to clear the air and come to terms with them. Although this is a painful undertaking, it is the basis for establishing an improved relationship between older parents and their children. Attempting to deny that uncomfortable emotions exist and avoiding a frank discussion of how they disrupt family relationships perpetuates problems that need to be addressed. On the other hand, family members can gain a clearer understanding of what is troubling them and correct misperceptions that are a source of conflict if they are willing to communicate and engage in a constructive examination of what stands in the way of developing more harmonious relationships.

Family therapy (sometimes in conjunction with individual psychotherapy) also helps family members deal with their own fear of growing old. Sons and daughters often deny that their parents are not physically vigorous or mentally alert. This denial grows out of fear about growing old themselves and represents an attempt to avoid having to face their own demise. As Barbara Silverstone and Kandel Hyman point out: "The feelings we have about our own old age often have a direct bearing on how effectively we can help our parents during their old age and how constructively we can plan for our own. People who have a generally positive attitude toward old age—including their own—are more likely to be able to reach out to their elderly parents with concern, compassion and constructive support. If old age appears as a time to be dreaded—and many features of modern society would suggest that it is—then our parents' decline may seem very threatening. Their aging seems to toll the bells for our own aging and our inevitable death" (1976, p. 27).

Solving Marital Problems

The physical and psychological changes that are associated with aging can have an adverse effect on the relationship between husbands and wives in late life. Some couples are plagued by problems that have not been resolved earlier and continue to be a source of conflict and dissatisfaction. However, some couples who have previously enjoyed a satisfactory and harmonious relationship begin to face serious problems after the husband has retired from a long and active career, as illustrated in the following examples:

Charles had always been generous and content with the way his wife ran the household, but after he retired his personality and his relation to his wife changed. He began to criticize the way she ran the home. When they shopped, he would put back things that Mary wanted, insisting that they were too expensive. He began to take over most of the household responsibilities, worked out a daily schedule and insisted it be carried out. Mary objected at first, but she had submitted to his dominating personality for so long that it was now a habit. She didn't have the strength to fight and prevent her husband from taking over what she considered to be her rightful territory.

In some cases, the wife is placed in the position of having to meet all the needs of her husband after retirement and begins to resent the demands he makes on her time and attention. As one wife put it: "John has made me his retirement hobby. He is more than a shadow. He has become my alter ego. He goes wherever I go and I seldom have a moment to myself. If I go shopping for clothes, he sits there until I am finished. I feel tense and can't shop leisurely as I'd like to do.

"Even in the house he wonders where I am if I have gone into another room, and he calls me. Sometimes I just hurriedly put on my coat and call to him that I am going on a necessary errand. It is my only escape, but when I return home, I find him sitting pathetically in front of the window waiting for my return. I can't help but feel guilty and sorry for him, but these feelings are always mixed with anger at the way my life is being controlled."

These cases illustrate how retirement can have a devastating effect on marriage, when husbands lose their sense of importance and have no territory of their own and begin to encroach on their wives' turf.

The feeling of goalessness that accompanies retirement can also have devastating consequences when the husband slips into a state of apathy and depression because he has no goal to pursue. As he becomes increasingly discontent, the husband may begin to blame his wife for the unhappy state of affairs. He may unfairly impose his own problems and dissatisfaction on his spouse as Leland Bradford, a retired psychologist, discovered when his wife, Martha, confronted him with his change in behavior and attitude:

Martha, clearly, directly, and withholding no punches, gave me a penetrating verbal picture of what I was like now, what I was doing to myself, and what I was doing to her. . . . She certainly alerted me to my drifting into goalessness. I could see my discontent quickly leading me into apathy and depression. The stirring-up helped me see how my failure in coping with my reverse in goals was adding to the burden of her own problems of adjustment. This did nothing to enhance my picture of myself as the competent, knowledgeable, supportive helping husband. I realized then that it was up to me to set challenges, goals and purpose for myself that would keep me an alert and active person (Pp. 34–36).

Counseling can help couples resolve the problem of goalessness and the effect it has on the marital relationship. Each partner may be assisted in defining new and different goals that give each of them a sense of personal identity that will be respected, heighten self-esteem and relieve the strain on the marital relationship.

Retirement does not always cause marital dissatisfaction. How well the marital partners are able to deal with the physical, psychological and social changes that accompany aging is also a critical factor. If one or both partners have developed rigid and incompromising ways of responding, they will have great difficulty making new responses and accommodation to changes in role and status. Rigid adherence to gender roles is also a deterrent to making an accommodation to changes that occur in late life. The husband who is willing to share household responsibilities that have fallen on his wife can make the transition less difficult if at the same time he does not usurp her territory against her will.

Older couples who have developed a network of friends and do not depend exclusively on each other for emotional support are more likely to have fewer problems in their marriage than those who have become locked into an overly dependent relationship from which they cannot escape. Marriage counseling and individual counseling may be helpful in moving partners to maintain their own identity in later years and achieve a degree in autonomy that is consistent with continued growth as they age. If both partners are able to maintain feelings of self-worth and have high self-esteem, they will probably have a satisfactory interpersonal relationship. Counseling can help them achieve and maintain a sense of integrity that will enrich and solidify the marital relationship.

Problem-Solving Approach

Communication difficulties are the most prevalent problems that married couples encounter. Partners complain that they can't discuss their differences without insulting each other or that they talk past each other and finally avoid any meaningful interaction because any attempt to resolve problems will result in frustration and disappointment.

A problem-solving approach can usually reduce or eliminate marital conflict. The steps involved in problem solving include: (1) recognizing that a problem exists; (2) agreement between the partners that they will try to work toward a solution; (3) identifying a specific and workable part of the problem to work on; (4) generating a number of alternative solutions; (5) selecting a certain solution to be implemented; (6) deciding on a course of action; (7) carrying out the action; and (8) reviewing the action.

During the initial interview, each partner is given an opportunity to "lay out" the problem or problems they believe need to be resolved. At this point, the problem is usually stated in the form of complaints. Each spouse will be inclined to become defensive as complaints are leveled at him or her. The session may become quite emotionally charged and the level of hostility may at times obscure any meaningful communication because of the strong emotional undertones. The couple may begin to flounder in their attempts to identify the problem that needs to be resolved.

The initial session gives the practitioner opportunity to point out that the way in which the couple has attempted to deal with difference and dissatisfaction in their relationship has proven to be unproductive and that they will need to develop a different approach to resolving problems. At this point, the practitioner may state what appears to be the major problems that are to be dealt with in future sessions. Both partners are asked if this statement accurately reflects the issues that need to be resolved. After this initial identification of problems to be worked on, the practitioner briefly outlines how future sessions will be conducted, explains that only one problem will be dealt with at a time, and that both partners will have an equal opportunity to state their views as to how the problem is to be resolved. Finally, the practitioner explains that he will not offer solutions but will help the couple reach a mutually satisfactory way of solving the problem.

In the next session, the practitioner reviews the problems that have been identified in the preceding interview and again asks the couple if the statement is accurate. At this point, one aspect of a general area of difficulty is examined in a systematic way. For example, one of the identified problems is "lack of communication," an issue raised by the wife. The practitioner asks the wife to define this "communication problem" more specifically to make sure that her husband understands what she means. The purpose is to make the problem manageable and to provide a model for communication that the couple can begin to follow in problem solving.

The temptation to explore the feelings that underlie problems should be avoided. Questions such as "And how does that make you feel?" will lead to a digression and will be unproductive at this point. The purpose is to engage the couple in listening to messages rather than responding through defensive maneuvers.

The practitioner then suggests that there may be several ways to solve the specific identified problem and that there are no right or wrong answers. The couple is required to consider these solutions until a mutually satisfactory way of coping with the problem is agreed upon. If no agreement can be reached, the couple may move on to a different identified problem using the same process of communication under the guidance of the practitioner.

The couple agrees to carry out the action that is required in the solution and to carefully note if the procedure has been followed. The couple reports whether the solution is "workable" in the following session. Modifications may be suggested if the proposal has not worked or the couple may want to consider the problem again and develop a different solution. In some cases, the practitioner may assist the couple in the problem-solving process, but only if they are unable to move ahead and permit the helper to contribute an opinion or present an alternative solution after the partners have made their own contributions. The couple is, of course, free to reject the option offered by the practitioner and there is no attempt to persuade them to adopt it.

Application and Evaluation

The problem-solving approach to the resolution of marital problems is relatively uncomplicated and straightforward. It is effective in marriage counseling that involves specific problems related to certain situations commonly found among the elderly: loss of physical health, impaired mental functioning and some forms of sexual dysfunctions. The problem-solving model is not appropriate in marital disturbances that arise out of deep-seated psychological internal conflict in one or both marital partners. A personality disorder in a husband or wife that results in acting out of hostile impulses is not amendable to the problem-solving approach in marriage counseling. However, this approach might be effective in helping the partner who is the target of hostility embark on a course of action that will avoid further destructive assaults from the spouse.

The outcome of marriage counseling depends on several factors. Problems that are of recent origin will respond more quickly than those that are long-standing and have characterized the marriage over an extended period. If both partners are aware of the need for help in resolving their problems, they will benefit more from counseling than if one of the spouses denies the existence of the difficulty and is resistant to using "outside help." Motivation is also a critical factor in the outcome of marriage counseling. If both partners place a high value on the relationship, they will be inclined to make the changes that are needed to maintain the marriage. If one or both partners enter counseling with the purpose of gaining some personal advantage, the outlook for any significant improvement in the marriage is bleak. The personality structure of the partners is also an important factor. Individuals who are highly rigid, who hold to unalterable views, and are unable to compromise in order to make the marriage work will be highly resistant to counseling.

Problem solving addresses one of the principle difficulties that are the source of marital dissatisfaction: the inability to communicate feelings openly and honestly. Ineffective communication results in unresolved conflict and unhappiness. The problem-solving approach offers an opportunity for both partners to overcome barriers to communication as they struggle with a satisfactory adjustment to the problems of aging.

Solving Sexual Problems

Dissatisfaction in sexual relations among older persons can be traced to several major factors. Sexual incompatability is often a result of other problems in the marital relationship and reflects unresolved hostility between the partners that interferes with maintaining harmonious and gratifying sexual activity. In helping couples cope with a problem in sexual adjustment, it is important to make a careful evaluation of their relationship outside the sexual area to determine if difficulties in interpersonal relationships is a barrier to sexual fulfillment. How the partners perceive themselves, how they perceive one another as persons, may give important clues to the disturbance in the sexual area.

Sexual dysfunctions can also be traced to inadequate and inaccurate information that creates anxiety and interferes with sexual functioning. An older man may actually frighten himself into impotency if he can't get an erection as quickly as he did during his youth. An older woman may blame her difficulty in achieving orgasm on the fact that she is aging and is therefore experiencing a decline in sexual interest that cannot be reversed. In most cases, couples who are misinformed are not aware how their negative attitudes toward themselves as attractive sex partners or negative attitudes toward the sexual act can be a hindrance to the enjoyment of sex. Men may measure their masculinity by their ability to bring their partners to orgasm. Women often feel they are at fault if they cannot achieve orgasm or arouse their partners. An inability to live up to these expectations is often regarded as failure and leads to a rapid decline in sexual activity and pleasure for both partners as they grow old.

Although impotence and a decline in sexual interest is a common complaint among older couples, this need not be an inevitable consequence of aging. Providing their health remains good, most couples can have pleasurable sexual relations. The main causes of unsatisfactory sexual adjustment among the elderly are not physiological but are a product of psychological reactions that interfere with sexual functioning.

Some sexual problems can be overcome if the couple understands gender differences in sexual functioning between men and women as they grow older. In the early years of marriage, the man's sexual needs are more urgent than his wife's, and her response is less rapid and intense. As they approach middle age, women's interest in sex increases, but while they retain their capacity to respond, they become less attractive than when they were young. On the other hand, the man's sexual desires gradually diminish, and his responses are slower and less intense with aging. Most couples are not aware of how these differences in sexual needs affect their relationship. Because they are unable to openly discuss the difference in their sexual makeup, they are unable to accommodate to changes in biological makeup as Helen Kaplan (1974) observes:

> Such couples can be helped if they recognize that normal age-related sexual changes exist, that they are not identical for husband and wife, that these changes are a product of biological rhythms and not of the quality of their love or attractiveness.... Couples can learn ways of

utilizing the differences and changes to enhance their closeness and to increase the pleasure and gratification they can give to one another. Lovemaking techniques can accommodate each partner's changing needs for stimulation and gratification, and the marriage can be enriched by a sensitive and mutually generous adaptation to each partner's age-related changes in sexual functioning. (P. 114.)

Sexual impotence in older men may be related to an intense fear of aging as in the case of Charles, age 64, who experienced what appeared to be sudden impotence. He was unable to sustain an erection for nine months, and his condition became an obsession. He was rapidly sinking into a depressed state.

Charles' wife was still ardent, but he could not achieve an erection with her. His inability to function triggered his anxiety about growing old. A complete physical examination showed that he was in good health, but Charles continued to believe that he would never be an adequate sexual partner. Questioning revealed that his impotence coincided with his retirement after a long and successful career. After a few months, he began to develop some hypochondriacal symptoms and showed great concern about his health.

In a conference with Charles and his wife, the therapist learned that their marriage had been very satisfactory and that their sexual adjustment had been good. Further exploration indicated that Charles had associated retirement with aging, and his self-image had undergone drastic change. The change involved a fear of growing old that had begun to seriously affect his sexual functioning.

In a discussion with the couple, the counselor pointed out that aging did bring about a normal decline in sexual drives in most men, but that the problem could be resolved. His wife was understanding and began to cooperate in stimulating Charles manually until he achieved an erection. Sexual pleasuring exercises increased the ease with which Charles responded to his wife's initiative within several weeks of counseling. As both partners learned to communicate their sexual needs and preferences, their sexual relationship was enhanced as they practiced new forms of sexual expression.

Many couples are too guilty or ashamed to admit that they are ignorant about sex, and they are too frightened to experiment when they find that they are sexually unresponsive. Men over fifty are used to having no problems achieving an erection in their youth. They do not realize that they need more intense stimulation as they grow older in order to function. A woman may not feel comfortable about asking her male partner to provide the kind of stimulation she wants because she fears he will reject her or consider her selfish. Unable to communicate, many couples remain silent and continue to have an unsatisfactory sexual life.

If the couple's sexual problem is due to sexual ignorance, the therapist can usually correct the situation by providing information about sexual techniques and explore more effective ways to stimulate sexual activity. Partners are encouraged to tell one another where and how they want to be caressed and are taught how to explore new ways of pleasuring their partners. They may give up the belief that the woman must always achieve orgasm, that the man should instantly and at all times be ready for coitus and that the partners must achieve orgasm simultaneously. Counseling that frees the couple from inaccurate perceptions about sexual functioning opens the door to a better sex life for many older couples who are temporarily having difficulty in their sexual adjustment.

The fear of failure is one of the major factors in sexual dysfunctioning in men. Once a man has failed to maintain an erection, he may begin to wonder if he is losing his sexual powers, focus his attention on the state of his erection and eventually has difficulty in performance. In counseling, the man is confronted with the adverse effect of his performance anxiety and how the role of being a spectator reduces his ability to have a normal, spontaneous erection. Self-observing behavior is a common cause of erectile difficulties and must be eliminated to restore adequate sexual functioning. In most cases, this habit of "spectatoring" can be overcome with a brief treatment that prevents the man from continuing to make self-judgments about his performance and helps him to lose himself in the spontaneous pleasure of lovemaking.

Failure to communicate openly about sexual feelings and needs is an important source of sexual dysfunctioning. Many couples could remedy their difficulties if they felt free to let each other know what pleases and what is a "turn off." A woman may remain non-orgasmic because she is afraid she will be rejected if she suggests more foreplay or tells her partner that clitoral stimulation excites her. She may be ashamed to tell him that she needs more time to reach orgasm and continues to simulate reaching a climax instead of correcting the problem. As Kaplan (1974) suggests, open communication may lead to changes in sexual interaction that is more satisfying.

It is extremely helpful to foster a system of open communication system between the lovers in such situations. He might be happy to stimulate her if he only knew what she needed. If she can risk telling him what she really feels, when the rejection she anticipates does not materialize, she feels closer and more loving and relaxed enough to reach a climax. (P. 134.)

The main purpose of sex therapy is to help couples deal with the obstacles that stand in the way of sexual satisfaction. In most cases, therapy is focused on the immediate causes of the dysfunctioning, such as spectatoring or fear of failure to perform adequately. Effecting changes in the sexual interaction by dealing with the "here and now" is often successful, even though it is not concerned with the deeper issues that create obstacles. Therapy is not directed toward questions such as "Why does the man persist in ruining his erection by spectatoring?" or "What experiences cause a woman to feel that she cannot ask her partner to stimulate her clitoris?"

The focus on the immediate cause can often help couples learn to function more adequately even though the root causes of their problems are not explored. When this approach is not effective, therapy is directed toward uncovering conflicts that are the intrapsychic causes of the problem and helping one or both partners resolve the conflict between wanting to enjoy sex and the unconscious fear of doing so. However, an extremely high proportion of sexually dysfunctional individuals, approximately 80 percent, can be free of their sexual problems without effecting changes in their basic personality structure or the dynamics of the marital relationship.

Sex Therapy Techniques

In most counseling situations, sex therapy is considered as a component of marital counseling and is directed toward problems due to lack of sexual information, breakdown in communication and conflict in the husband-wife relationship. Couples who are seen in these settings are amenable to brief therapy. Those couples whose problems stem from deep unconscious feelings of insecurity or who are involved in intense marital conflict are not appropriate candidates and require more intensive, long-term psychotherapy.

Most brief procedures for the treatment of sexual dysfunctions rely heavily on the use of prescribed sexual experiences. Masters and Johnson pioneered in developing a highly effective regimen of sexual tasks that were prescribed to shift the couple's attention away from erection and orgasm and focus attention on erotic feeling. Sexual exercises were prescribed for treatment of specific problems, including the "squeeze method" for premature ejaculation and various coital positions and techniques for genital stimulation of the male and female. These apparently simple exercises have been found to be effective in modifying destructive sexual behavior and help the couple learn to make love in new and more enjoyable ways.

The application of these sexual tasks to problems of men who are troubled by erectile failure begins with sensate focus exercises, starting with non-genital contacts followed by manual stimulation of the man's genital area. After the man has achieved an erection, the woman is instructed to use a teasing technique while she is in the superior position. If the man loses his erection, the woman repeats the teasing technique until he has another erection. No time pressure is put on the man to achieve an erection, and efforts are directed toward avoiding fear of performance failure. The purpose is to enable the man to become sexually aroused in a normal, relaxed way. Since older men do not achieve erection without the cooperation of the wife in providing manual stimulation to the penis, the use of this technique can be appropriately used in therapy with older couples when combined with an explanation of why this procedure is helpful.

As Masters and Johnson point out, secondary impotence in older men is due to "psychogenic blocking" that prevents them from reaching orgasm because they believe they are impotent even though they are physiologically capable of adequate sexual functioning. They conclude: "If the aging male does not succeed in talking himself out of effective sexual functioning by worrying about the physiological factors in his sexual response patterns altered by the aging process, if his peers do not destroy his sexual confidence, if he and his partner maintain a reasonably good state of health, he certainly can and should continue unencumbered sexual functioning indefinitely" (p. 326).

Sensate focus or pleasuring exercises are useful in enhancing the couple's sexual relation. Sensate focus, originally developed by Masters and Johnson, provides a non-demanding atmosphere that encourages natural sexual feelings and responses to emerge. Non-demand pleasuring experiences involve genital stimulation and non-demand coitus, beginning with sensate focus. Sensate focus consists of having the couple forego sexual intercourse for a period of time and limiting their activity to gentle touching and caressing each other's bodies. Both concentrate on the pleasure they derive from non-genital touching. This exercise is especially effective in arousing sensuous and erotic responses in the woman and is followed by genital stimulation of her breasts, clitoral area and vaginal entrance. The genital stimulation increases the woman's sexual responsiveness and she is eager to go on to the next exercise.

The non-demand exercise is initiated by the woman who is in control of the coital thrusting as she inserts the man's penis and paces the movements to suit her own desire. The teasing and leisurely lovemaking is usually highly exciting because she can experience unimpeded sexual pleasure. The man is instructed to not reach orgasm during this exercise. The woman is instructed to "be selfish" and think only of her own sensations without concern about bringing her partner to orgasm.

These exercises are not meant to be mere mechanical devices but are used by the therapist to determine what is standing in the way of sexual fulfillment. The couple's reactions to the exercises is discussed, and difficulties that either partner encounters in carrying out the sexual tasks are carefully reviewed to help the couple resolve conflicts and feelings that inhibit sexual response. Communication between the partners in which they exchange reactions to the experience helps them resolve the problems they have encountered in their sexual relationship and leads to more satisfying lovemaking.

Sex and Health

Many physical illnesses can have an adverse effect on sexual functioning, and although the most frequent causes of sexual disorder are psychological, physical factors should be ruled out before sex therapy is undertaken. Only about 10 percent of dysfunctional sex problems involve physical factors. Illness, psychological states such as drug ingestion, depression and fatigue have an adverse effect on both men and women. Men who have erectile problems may be suffering from undetected diabetes, multiple sclerosis, or have a low testosterone level. Abuse of alcohol, taking narcotics or medication for hypertension can also be significant causes of impotence. Loss of sexual interest may be due to a debilitating disease such as hepatitis or be the result of depression.

Females' sexual functioning can also be affected by physical factors. General loss of interest or unresponsiveness in sex can be caused by illness, depression or use of certain drugs. An abrupt decline in estrogen and progesterone results in some constriction of the vaginal barrel, loss of thickness in the muscular lining of the vagina and a reduction in vaginal lubrication. The clitoris may be somewhat smaller in older women, but this does not interfere with her ability to enjoy sexual intercourse if she is properly stimulated by her partner. If her lubrication capacity is inadequate, a vaginal lubricant used before intercourse prevents discomfort.

Women who have had opportunities for regular and satisfying sexual experience in the past are likely to derive pleasure from intercourse long past age 65. Women tend to want more, rather than less, sex as they approach middle age and beyond, and their responsiveness is only slightly less rapid or intense. An increase in libido after menopause and a peak in the sexual drive in women in middle age may be attributed to having learned how to achieve greater satisfaction with the use of sexual techniques that meet the special needs of women.

Changes in sexual capacity or sexual interest is not the principle reason for a cessation of sexual activity in the older population. The most important impediment to a continued involvement in sex among the elderly may well be the attitude of society that sex should be discouraged and disapproved when individuals reach their sixtieth or sixty-fifth birthday. Americans generally regard sexuality as the prerogative of the young. Older persons are expected to have no need for or interest in sexual gratification. This uninformed attitude may prevent many older men and women from enjoying an important source of sensual pleasure that is not a monopoly of youth.

As Ruth Weg (1976) points out: "Society bestows the meaning and power of sexual expression. The societally endowed power of sexuality has been identified with the vitality and desirability of youth. Middle-aged and older persons can accept, however grudgingly, the inefficiency of the organic system, but the first signs of natural aging in the reproductive system are a threat to identity and an awesome reminder of the rolelessness and sexlessness ahead that society has predicted" (p. 218).

Summary

Family therapy, marriage counseling and sex therapy are important methods of helping older persons cope with emotional problems and deal with critical life situations that require an accommodation on the part of family members and marital partners. All three models of intervention are similar, in that they are not aimed at effecting changes in the client's personality but are geared to changing interpersonal relationships. Family therapy attempts to alter relationships between parents and adult children. Problem-oriented marriage counseling attempts to improve relationships between spouses. Sex therapy attempts to bring about changes in the way sexual partners relate to one another in one or more areas of sexual interaction.

Although these models of intervention are somewhat limited in working with older persons, they also hold promise in resolving emotional problems that involve relationships between elderly clients and significant others in their environment.

Chapter 7

WORKING WITH GROUPS

Group therapy to help older persons cope with the emotional and mental problems includes a variety of approaches: group psychotherapy, behavior modification, and cognitive therapy, reminiscing groups, remotivation and reality groups, music and art therapy and self-help programs. Because older persons have special emotional problems and are often more vulnerable than younger individuals, the group process provides much needed encouragement and empathy to group members and helps them cope with emotional difficulties more effectively.

The group process can be used effectively in community or institutional settings. The group process carries out the following functions: (a) provides a supporting network for the members; (b) reduces social isolation; (c) encourages self-expression; (d) increases self-esteem; and (e) helps group members gain new insight into the nature of their problems.

Reducing Social Isolation. The group experience breaks down feelings of isolation that is common among the elderly. For the first time, they may realize that they are not alone in facing problems. By listening to other group members, they begin to find relief from feelings of loneliness that often lead to depression. Older persons also begin to develop confidence in their ability to relate to others in social situations and improve skills in interpersonal relationships. By learning to communicate and interact, they overcome a tendency to withdraw and are able to form connections with other group members. For older persons who are left without the support and companionship of a mate and for those who have little opportunity for social contact, the group experience is not only beneficial but most welcome.

Providing Support. Many older persons face situations that involve stress and anxiety. The group can offer the support they need to help them through difficult events that involve significant losses. The group provides a sense of belonging that enables the elderly to function more adequately as they begin to solve problems and deal with difficult situations with the help of others. As they see other older persons cope with emotional problems successfully, they also gain confidence in their ability to do the same and make progress in solving their own problems. The experience of others who have been in similar situations is living proof that problems can be overcome.

Providing Models. The group experience not only provides support; it also shows the individual members how they can change their behavior. Most group members are eager to pass on to others what they have learned. Older persons who have found ways to become more assertive can help those who have difficulty forming new friendships. The techniques of modeling behavior to demonstrate new ways of behaving are very useful tools to helping older persons, especially if followed by behavior rehearsal that reinforces new ways of behaving in certain situations. Role playing gives members an opportunity to try out new behavior patterns and apply them to actual life situations outside the group.

Encouraging Self-Expression. Group therapy provides a safe way for older persons to express feelings that they are reluctant to reveal in other settings. Free expression is often a new experience for some, especially those who have been censored when they expressed hostility or anger or tried to show positive feelings of affection and tenderness. The group experience brings many suppressed feelings into conscious awareness and helps older persons integrate them into their lives. Group members learn that others will accept expressions of feelings and that the results will not be disastrous if they display emotions more openly and honestly.

Increasing Self-Esteem. Many older persons perceive themselves as inadequate and lack feelings of self-worth. The group experience can be effective in helping them improve their self-image and increase their self-confidence. Those who feel inadequate may be perceived by other group members as having assets that are valuable and useful. Being considered a valid member of a group enhances the individual's perception of himself as a person of some importance. Moreover, as older persons begin to help others in the group solve problems and cope with emotional difficulties, they gain a strong sense of value because they are contributing to the group process. The member who is helped also gains from this experience because he feels that other persons regard him as being worthy of their attention and are willing to extend themselves in his behalf.

Developing Insight. The group process helps members become aware of the motives and reasons that underlie their own behavior as they observe other group members in the course of group therapy. Each member begins to analyze his own reactions to certain situations that are anxiety-provoking. Some events from the past may have created feelings that are unresolved and need to be re-examined in the group process. Reminiscing group therapy has proven useful in helping older persons integrate experiences and feelings that have their origin in earlier life and makes it possible for them to achieve what Erikson has called "a stage of integrity." The development of insight is usually not consciously sought in the group process, but it often develops spontaneously out of the give-and-take among group members.

Planning Group Therapy

A group goes through various stages before the members develop a sense of "we-ness" that binds them together and makes the group experience meaningful. In the initial phase, the group leader focuses on the following basic processes: orienting members as to the purpose of the group, establishing the norms or rules of the group and establishing a trusting relation among the members.

Defining Purpose. It is important to inform the members why the group is being formed and give ample opportunity for individuals to state their own reasons for joining the group and how they expect to benefit from the experience. The purpose must relate to specific problems and set out definite goals. For example, "I want to overcome my fear of being alone," or "I want to find some reason for living." The purpose of the individual group members must be integrated into the overall purpose of the group. If the purpose is stated in terms of what the members expect to accomplish, everyone becomes aware of how the group process can contribute to achieving individual goals.

Contracting. Once the purpose of individual and group goals has been defined, each member negotiates a contract that spells out what obligations are involved in joining the group. In most cases, this contract can be formulated in a simple and forthright statement as to the length of time the members will give to the group, number of sessions, length of session and attendance requirements. In working with older persons, the contract is usually kept uncomplicated and put in terms that can be clearly understood. Contracting helps clear up any misunderstandings at the outset and assures the leader that those who join the group are committed to its purpose.

Group Norms. When individuals join the group, they usually do not know what to expect in terms of behavior. Setting norms or rules therefore becomes an important task for the therapist to complete early in the life of the group. Rules about communication can be spelled out: Who is permitted to speak? What subjects, if any, are out of bounds? Are members to address messages to the therapist or to other group members? How much disagreement is to be tolerated? What are the rights of each individual? Are absences to be excused? If so, under what circumstances? Clarifying these questions as soon as possible will help the group to have a sense of stability that is essential to progress in therapy.

Developing Trust. Most older persons are somewhat uncomfortable and anxious when they enter the group for the first time. They are concerned about whether they will be liked and accepted by other members and wonder if they can confide in them and relate to them openly and honestly. The group leader can reduce their anxiety by explaining that the experience is new and that it is understandable that they are uncertain and hesitant to form a trusting relationship with others. By creating an atmosphere that invites trust, the barriers to forming such relationships will gradually be overcome. Some members may fear that their right to privacy will be violated. Setting a firm rule that what is said within the group sessions is confidential and that what happens will not be revealed to persons outside the group leads to a relationship of trust.

The Group Leader's Tasks

The group leader plays an important role in helping members achieve their goals and benefit from the group process. The principal activities in which the leader engages include: (1) providing support to individual group members and the group as a whole; (2) making communication and interaction among group members effective; (3) helping members see their life situation more realistically; (4) enabling them to deal with problems and cope with emotionally traumatic events; and (5) applying specific techniques that will be effective in certain given situations.

Supporting Strategies. Encouraging feelings of self-esteem and competence among older persons is an important objective in working with older persons. Several strategies can be employed to bring about this result. The leader can convey the feeling that all persons in the group are worthy of attention and recognize each individual's need for acceptance and support. Group members also benefit from empathetic responses that indicate an understanding of what an older person is undergoing and an appreciation of the feelings that are involved. False expressions such as "I know" are not likely to be helpful, but the leader can achieve good results by saying: "I really don't understand, but maybe you can help me know what it feels like to be in your situation." Paying attention to what members say is in and of itself an indication that the leader wants to be helpful and cares. This supportive strategy is particularly beneficial, because older persons are often ignored and their thoughts and feelings are not taken seriously.

Facilitating Group Interaction. When the group is in the beginning phase of therapy, members lack skills in the art of communication and cannot effectively express thoughts or feelings. The leader can help members develop skills in interpersonal relations by facilitating interaction and communication through the use of several strategies. The leader can restate an expression of feeling by a group member and check out whether the perception is accurate or whether the individual wants to convey a different feeling. By "checking out" the meaning of what members are saying, other individuals become aware that messages need to be clarified so that the intention is not misunderstood. As members listen to one another, they usually find that there is a central theme to which they can relate and the leader can use this as an opportunity to encourage further exchanges among the group. For example, a statement such as, "I sense that everyone is feeling discouraged," can help members recognize that they are trying to express similar feelings and states of mind.

The leader can also become aware that non-verbal forms of communication are being used by group members to express anxiety, hostility or other forms of psychological discomfort. Group members may not openly express hostility in verbal communication, because they are seen as improper or threatening. As the interaction among the members unfolds, the leader can discover blocks to communication and call them to the attention of the group. If the group can deal with these barriers in the early phase of therapy openly and honestly, progress will be accelerated and the stability of the group will be enhanced.

Confronting Reality. There are times when group members need to confront reality and recognize that faulty perceptions about themselves, about other persons or about their life situation interferes with their ability to solve emotional difficulties. When this occurs, the leader may be called upon to confront this faulty perception by pointing out that irrational thinking leads to self-destructive behavior. The techniques that have been described in the section on cognitive therapy are useful in helping group members become aware of how irrational thinking brings about emotional distress and causes anxiety, depression and other serious psychological problems.

Confrontation must be used rather cautiously in working with older persons. If accompanied by expressions of empathy, they usually realize that they are not being attacked and are more open to reviewing thoughts, feelings, and perceptions in a more realistic way. A less threatening form of confrontation may be used, such as saying: "People often see things in different ways. Let's see what is going on and take a good look at it once again."

Some group members can recognize that their behavior and attitudes had their origin in the past and have been carried over into the present. This form of insight may be quite useful once it has been pointed out that dysfunctional behavior and faulty thinking can be corrected. The leader needs to be aware when they have reached the point that they are ready to confront reality. If they are involved in looking at their behavior objectively and are trying to understand the reasons for it, confrontation and interpretation will be effective.

Achieving Competence. Older persons are often concerned about their physical and mental competence as the aging process begins to diminish their physical vigor and their ability to cope with problems. The group process can serve to significantly improve the ability of older persons to solve a variety of problems that older people confront. The leader can encourage members to report situations that have given them difficulty and ask the group to discuss various ways in which the matter could be resolved. There is a strong probability that many in the group will have experienced similar problems, have found ways of dealing with them and can provide helpful suggestions.

In some cases, the leader can supply useful information that individual members of the group as a whole can use. An educational approach can be a vital part of the group process, because there are many areas in which older persons lack knowledge and information in regard to health services, social services and community programs that are designed to help older persons. In some areas, self-help groups are available to work on specific problems such as retirement, widowhood, Alzheimer's disease and other concerns of the elderly. Referral to such groups may be considered in situations where conveying information is the primary need. However, the main objective in working with groups is to develop basic skills in problem solving, rather than finding specific answers to specific situations. The techniques used to develop problem-solving skills have been described in a previous chapter and include: identifying problems, establishing priorities among problems, considering alternative solutions and carrying out tasks that are necessary to implement the solution. If group members can acquire these skills in problem solving, they can apply them to a wide range of situations that accompany the aging process.

Choosing a Therapeutic Approach. A number of approaches to group intervention are available and each has a somewhat distinct objective and methodology. The leader can determine whether one given approach or a combination of various intervention methods is appropriate to achieve a given set of objectives. Behavior modification can be used in a number of situations such as systematic desensitization to treat anxiety or assertive training to promote changes in interpersonal relations. Cognitive therapy can be useful in helping depressed persons by identifying and correcting faulty perceptions and irrational thinking. Various forms of humanistically oriented groups are effective in enhancing self-image and creating a strong sense of self-worth. Reminiscing therapy has been found useful in helping older persons face impending death. Creative and artistic expression groups have important rehabilitative and enhancement results. Self-help groups also serve a special purpose in helping older persons cope with specific problems such as widowhood, retirement, alcohol addiction and drug abuse. Behavior modification, problem solving and cognitive therapy have already been described and the techniques employed in these approaches can be used in working with groups. Various other approaches will be described in the material that follows.

Psychotherapy Groups

The traditional form of psychotherapy that is aimed at a restructuring of personality through developing insight is not useful in working with older persons. Instead, the therapist uses the group process to help members deal with the "here and now" rather than focusing on the unconscious conflicts that may have created emotional difficulties. By providing emotional support, psychotherapy makes it less difficult for members to cope with losses and continue to function at an acceptable level. Emphasis is placed on present problems and developing an understanding of how emotional problems can be resolved.

Five areas need to be considered in forming a psychotherapeutic group: (1) purpose of the therapy; (2) group composition; (3) group goals; (4) leadership; and (5) practical considerations.

Purpose. The purpose of group psychotherapy is to encourage communication among the members themselves to resolve emotional problems. The most common concerns that emerge in the group sessions include: (1) depression and thoughts of suicide; (2) developing new roles in later life; and (3) difficulties in social relationships. The most common concerns expressed by group members center around loss of the work role, loss of dignity, loss of physical and intellectual capacity, and loss of family and friends. Being able to talk about these losses is especially beneficial, because it is easier to express emotions in the presence of other group members with whom there is a positive, accepting relation. Simply knowing that there is a group especially and exclusively meant for them gives older persons a sense of self-worth. Through interacting with peers, group therapy provides an opportunity to develop a positive self-image, serves as an outlet for expression of feeling and offers answers to important questions, as Judith Altholz (1984) points out:

> Only rarely can older people meet together in a group to discuss their feelings, concerns and difficulties. Group psychotherapy offers the chance to discuss common problems and the alternative solutions discovered by older people. It can also offer an answer to the question many older people ask themselves: "Now that I am old, what kind of person am I supposed to be?" (P. 255).

Group Composition. A psychiatric diagnosis can be an important consideration in determining if an older person should be included in a psychotherapeutic group. If all members are diagnosed as having a withdrawn depression, there is a strong likelihood that the group will not make much progress because there is not enough energy or ability to verbalize. The most obvious criterion for selecting group members is their ability to communicate their thoughts and feelings, because a successful outcome depends upon active verbal exchanges and emotional responses among group members. Older persons who are suffering from serious hearing loss are usually not suitable candidates for group psychotherapy. They will feel isolated because they are unable to participate in the group process.

Uncontrolled psychotics are difficult to handle in psychotherapeutic groups, and their presence disturbs other group members. Some leaders find that hypochondriacal persons should be excluded because of their tendency to center group discussion on their symptoms and prevent the group's giving attention to other problems.

Group Goals. Ensuring that the members understand the goal of a therapeutic group is an important factor in the beginning phase of working with older persons. For example, they may be informed that the goal is to help members become less anxious or to help people cope with grief. In developing goals, individual group members should be encouraged to help formulate the group goals and also asked to state what they expect to gain from participating in the group. Out of this exchange, the group can make a "blend" between the goals of individual members and the goals of the group as a whole. After the goals have been clearly stated and understood, prospective members can decide if they can make a firm commitment to join the group, attend sessions regularly and participate in the group process. In some cases, a brief written contract may be obtained, setting out the goals and a commitment from each member in order to reduce the possibility of misunderstanding of what is involved.

Group Leadership. Most psychotherapeutic groups have dual leadership, and often a psychiatrist and a social worker are chosen to lead the group to provide a model of complimentary roles in which each plays an important, but somewhat different, role. The leaders must determine beforehand what role or roles they want to assume in regard to being active or passive or in shifting roles at various points in the group process. One leader may be the target of the group's aggressive feelings and the other may act as facilitator or comforter.

There are several advantages to working with a co-therapist. Because the psychotherapeutic process involves complex interactions between therapist and group members, the demands are greater than in individual therapy, as Raymond Poggi points out:

> Working with a co-therapist permits me to sit back and relax and turn things over when I'm puzzled about events in the group or about my feelings or when I'm just plain tired. I can rely on my "friend" to spot my unusual behavior and, in so doing, help me spot my countertransference responses sooner than I might do on my own. Together we can spot out particularly difficult situations and support one another's efforts. (P. 363.)

To develop effective leadership, the co-therapists must work together closely. Frequent mettings between them are necessary to discuss any problems in the working relationship and to plan ahead to coordinate their efforts, decide on strategy, and determine goals. These discussions provide a valuable basis for evaluating the group's progress and planning intervention techniques in particular situations that arise during the course of therapy.

Practical Considerations. Several practical matters must be considered when embarking on a group therapy project. Suitable space and facilities must be made available and transportation problems must be resolved in advance to avoid the likelihood of frequent absences from group meetings. The length of the sessions must be determined, taking into account the energy level of the participants. The physical environment of the meeting place is very important for older persons. They cannot very well tolerate extreme temperatures, noisy intercoms and other forms of distraction. Meeting times are also an important consideration. Evening meetings are usually not acceptable, because older persons may be afraid to be out after dark. Morning meetings are usually not the best time for working with depressed patients, and scheduling of the group sessions should be based on when the members will be functioning best. Physical ailments are common among the elderly and allowance must be made so as to accommodate their limitations. Because many older persons who could benefit from group therapy are poor and cannot afford to pay for transportation, special plans must be made for them to attend the sessions.

Humanistic Group Therapy

The humanistic approach to group therapy with older persons represents a departure from other modalities. Psychoanalytic therapy is based on the theory that emotional problems are the result of unconscious inner conflicts and that, through free association and dream interpretation, these conflicts can be resolved. Behavioral therapy regards emotional problems as manifestation of maladaptive behavior that can be eliminated by applying appropriate techniques to modify or eliminate the undesired behavior. Cognitive therapy is based on the premise that irrational thinking and distorted perceptions are at the root of emotional difficulties and holds that if they are replaced by rational, realistic thinking, emotional problems will be resolved.

Humanistic approaches do not attempt to seek out unconscious motivations, identify maladaptive behavior or clarify faulty thinking. The humanistic therapist is primarily interested in the whole person and seeks to help people reach a stage of what Maslow has called **self-actualization,** i.e. functioning at the height of one's creative, affective and intellectual ability. The characteristics of self-actualization include acceptance of others, acceptance of self, the capacity for meaningful relationships, spontaniety, autonomy and inner-directedness.

Among the various forms of humanistic psychology is **client-centered** therapy developed by Carl Rogers. This approach focuses less on specific problems and solutions and helps clients develop strong feelings of self-worth to eliminate anxiety, depression and other emotional difficulties. To achieve this goal, the therapist uses the principle of congruence, unconditioned positive regard, acceptance and accurate empathetic understanding. By exploring the client's inner life and providing a relationship of positive regard, people are enabled to grow into a higher level of understanding about themselves and manage their lives more effectively. Although many problems of the elderly usually require more directive methods of intervention, this approach does meet an important need for emotional support and a meaningful relationship with the therapist. Client-centered therapy is useful in helping clients sort out their feelings to events that have occurred in their past and also plays an important part in enriching their present life.

Gestalt therapy developed by Fritz Perls is also a form of humanistic therapy but differs from client-centered therapy in its emphasis on the "here and now" that forces the client to become aware of feelings, even those that are uncomfortable. The mental health practitioner's task is to ask the client to "stay with the feeling, confront and explore it and experience it completely in order to gain better understanding of self and relationships to others." Various techniques are employed to elicit strong feelings, including exaggeration of certain verbal or body language cues, acting out unfinished business, and dream work, and role playing.

Several types of workshops and growth groups with older persons have been employed to enrich experience of the members rather than eradicate mental illness. Gestalt groups stage or structure exercises to promote personal growth and improve interpersonal relationships by feedback from group members who observe their behavior. Among the events that promote change or reduce blocks to growth are the following:

- Observing other group members having meaningful emotional experiences.
- Gaining perspective on one's problems by exchange of ideas.
- Self-disclosure, appreciating that others have similar problems and sharing personal feelings that are not usually expressed.
- Experimenting with new behavior and receiving feedback from others.
- Achieving insight into one's own behavior or problems. In order for change to occur in growth groups, both disclosure and insight are critical.

There is some evidence to suggest that older persons can benefit from a humanistic group experience. Learning exercises need to be slower-paced where non-verbal communication is involved, but some older persons may be able to participate in these forms of group interaction.

A project using a humanistic approach with the elderly was conducted by SAGE (Senior Actualization and Growth Experience). The purpose was to "utilize the minds, bodies and spirits of its older participants." The techniques employed included deep relaxation, sensory awareness, Gestalt techniques, communication exercises, and biofeedback. The project also used the Gestalt "empty chair" exercise to help members cope with death and mourning and deal with "unfinished business." The SAGE project improved self-esteem and alleviated depression.

Group Reminiscing Therapy

Reminiscing is characteristic of later life and serves as a way of adapting to the aging process. Memory of past events establishes a sense of continuity for older persons and enables them to maintain a consistent sense of personal identity that might otherwise be lost. Studies by McMahon and Rhudick also indicate that reminiscing in group therapy increases enjoyment of social relations and can promote an understanding of the relationship between generations (McMahon, 1964).

Butler and Lewis also found that reminiscence is a normal "life review process" that can be a helpful tool in resolving past conflict and integrate them to give new significance to past events. Butler describes life review as "the progressive return of consciousness of past experience and particularly the resurgence of unresolved conflicts" and suggests that reminiscence maintains self-esteem by giving aged persons a sense of accomplishment (Butler, 1963).

The impact of reminiscing therapy on two groups of depressed elders that met for one-half hour per week for eight consecutive weeks is described by Mary Ann Matteson (1984). She found that there was significant improvement in those who participated in the programs. Reminiscing about past achievements and accomplishments brought about pride in what they had done and provided a structure for greater social interaction and the formation of new relationships among group members (p. 292). Many who had been sullen and withdrawn at the beginning of the eight sessions were more outgoing and were more involved in social interaction at the end of the group experience.

Reminiscing therapy is effective for older persons who were previously active and enjoyed persons but experience loss in competency as they grow old. The losses of old age pose a threat to some older persons, and reminiscence provides an ego support that restores a feeling of self-worth. In a sense, reminiscence is a defense mechanism that can be used against aging. The value of maintaining a consistent self-image has been found to be an important factor in adjusting to change among older persons. S. S. Tobin (1971) concludes that as the elderly become more psychologically disengaged, they strive to reaffirm who they are and are able to define themselves as unique and special persons who are worthy of respect.

Jean Kiermet's (1984) experiment in reminiscing therapy with 23 residents of a nursing home indicates that it can be especially useful in working with depressed persons who have a special need to recall their past experiences. "The institutionalized elderly, as a group, experience considerable personal and environmental stress," she writes. "Their concepts of themselves as competent individuals are challenged by decreasing physical and mental skills, or both, and the loss of meaningful personal relationships. It may be very difficult for them to remember that they have ever been loved or that they have done anything worthwhile" (p. 301).

Participating in reminiscing therapy is both fun and educational for the group leaders themselves. As older persons in the group recall past events, the leader learns much about the lives of individual group members. In a sense, the leader becomes the learner as the group members provide significant material from their personal experience. Reminiscing is also a method of stimulating older persons to use the life review process to integrate their lives and achieve a sense of completeness that is important to their emotional well-being.

To insure a beneficial outcome, reminiscence therapy needs to be based on an identifiable structure. Otherwise, group sessions will deteriorate into simply talking about the "good old days" and the group will not make progress toward achieving the goals of therapy. One example of structuring life review is offered by Ryden (1981), who suggests the following four guidelines:

1. Initiate reminiscence by using open-ended questions or by involving the group members in activities that lead to reminiscence.
2. Reinforce reminiscence by giving praise or non-verbal approval when members express appropriate material.
3. Helping members cope with the feelings that are involved when they recall specific events that are especially meaningful.
4. Helping family members cope with the reminiscence process itself and to deal with the emotions that are provoked in making a life review.

Another approach is suggested by Frey (1983), who found that depressive symptoms could be diminished by using a highly structured method in making life reviews. The approach involved these steps:

1. Both positive and negative feelings should be related to the event being discussed.
2. Reactions of the individual to other persons involved in the event should be explored.
3. Thoughts and images that come to mind when reminiscing should be related to the event.
4. Hopes, anxieties and fears should be related to the event.
5. Unresolved feelings of guilt, anger or a desire to avoid others should be related to the event.

These more structured approaches give the group members specific tools that they can use to work on their current emotional problems by relating the present to the past in a meaningful way.

Because reminiscence is flexible and easy to apply, it can be used in a variety of groups to improve self-esteem and provide positive roles for older persons in institutional long-term care. However, there are potential dangers. Unpleasant memories may be stirred up in reminiscent therapy and not be resolved unless the therapist takes time to help the group deal with these traumatic events by instilling hope, and enabling members to take a new perspective on the past and gain a sense of confidence in their ability to cope with current difficulties. Several options are available to counteract negative aspects of life review: comforting, deepening the feeling or moving away from the disturbing reminiscence. Each case must be evaluated on the needs of the individual group member. Some need to be comforted. Others need to express their feelings. Still others need to distance themselves from a traumatic event that is overwhelming. If the group therapist has made a careful evaluation of each member's personality and emotional needs, these negative reactions can be dealt with appropriately and bring about the desired therapeutic effect.

Assertion Training Groups

Assertion training is beginning to be used to help older persons to speak up for what they want and what they need because the pattern of passive behavior is often associated with aging. Assertion training may be offered on an individual basis, but there are advantages to a group approach that permits an opportunity for older persons to support one another as they practice assertive behavior and participate in exercises that stimulate and enforce new forms of response to specific situations that are encountered in daily living. The use of role playing, modeling and feedback gives a concrete demonstration of how behavior can be changed and how faulty and irrational thinking interferes with assertiveness. Older persons can benefit from these exercises by reshaping their thinking and enlarging their behavior repertoire.

Assertion training, unlike some treatment modes, may include both behavioral and cognitive components. A cognitive-behavioral approach is based on the premise that people's thinking influences the way they feel and behave. To help people identify patterns of thinking that inhibit self-assertion, this model includes four stages of intervention:

1. Development of a high regard for one's own personal rights
2. Discrimination between arrestive and aggressive behavior.
3. Restructuring one's thinking in specific situations
4. Rehearsal of assertive responses and behavior.

Group approaches in assertion training is used to train participants to move through these four stages and may be structured in the following manner:

Session One: Positive Assertion and Non-Verbal Behaviors. In this session, group members introduce themselves and are asked to identify the behaviors they would like to change. They are also encouraged to give and receive compliments and make positive statements about themselves. Group members usually are able to recognize that they have thoughts that prevent them from acting assertively and may often state, "I can't say good things about myself because people will think I am bragging."

Session Two: Personal Rights and Discrimination Training. This session focuses on what members of the group believe to be their personal rights. One method of helping the group is to list all the rights to which they think they are entitled, such as:

1. The right to express your beliefs, ideas, desires and feelings.
2. The right to decide how to use one's time.
3. The right to decide what to do with your body.
4. The right to decide what to do with your property.

After the group has completed this exercise, the leader shows how these rights are often violated and gives specific examples to which the group can respond.

A second task to be performed by the group is designed to enable members to distinguish between non-assertive, assertive and aggressive behavior. Emphasis is placed on the right to refuse to answer positively to requests from others and to assess how faulty thinking patterns interfere with acting assertively, such as feeling responsible for how others feel if a request is denied.

Session Three: Cognitive Restructuring. In this session, the trainer teaches participants to recognize how irrational thoughts prevent people from acting assertively. Members are asked to note that most of their irrational beliefs about acting assertively are obsolete and catastrophic in character, such as "I must," "I need," "I've got to." The trainer then provides specific techniques for changing the content of these irrational thoughts and "internal dialogues." Participants then learn to challenge irrational or faulty thinking and substitute more rational realistic thoughts.

Session Four: Behavioral Rehearsal. This session focuses on specific types of situations in which assertive behavior is involved: (a) situations in which someone is doing something that hurts you; (b) making and refusing requests without feeling guilty; and (c) dealing with persons who are overly persistent. Exercise formats may be used by the trainer which include asking participants to act out roles that demonstrate how to refuse requests assertively. Group members may coach one another at any point by suggesting improvements that might be made to cope with a given situation.

Participants in assertion training are encouraged to engage in out-of-group activity to solidify the gains they have made. The trainer may ask members to discuss what happened when they worked on a specific situation outside the group.

Techniques of cognitive-behavioral assertion training can be effectively employed in groups. In a group situation, several group members can query and contradict the faulty thinking and behavior of an individual. The impact is likely to be greater than that of a single therapist in changing thinking and behavior. Other advantages that the group experience provides include these:

1. The group is a laboratory where emotional and behavioral patterns of an individual can be directly observed and commented on by other group members.
2. In the group process, people can see that they are not alone in having problems in assertiveness and that they need not condemn themselves for having disturbance-creating ideas.
3. The group provides an opportunity to practice assertive behavior and the participants learn by doing.
4. Individuals can observe the progress other members are making and see that the techniques of assertive behavior are effective and that they, too, can change.
5. Revealing thoughts and feelings in a group may be quite helpful because they recognize that nothing is quite as shameful as they might have thought it was.
6. People get valuable feedback from the group. "They begin to see themselves more and more as others see them, to see some of the poor or wrong impressions they make on others, and learn how to change some of their behaviors," observes Albert Ellis (1977, p. 276).

In selecting older persons for assertion training, it is necessary to exclude those who are cognitively impaired because only persons who are able to monitor their thoughts can benefit by this approach.

Other Group Interventions

Self-Help Groups. Self-help groups have been in existence for a long time and are worth considering as a useful method of helping older persons cope with a wide range of problems. They can best be described as "the practice of activities that individuals personally initiated and perform on their own behalf in maintaining life, health and well-being. Although these groups are carried on by lay persons, professionals have been active in founding, supporting and offering consultation to them. Self-support groups are usually formed by peers who come together to satisfy a common need or cope with specific problems such as feelings about widowhood, loss of the work role, loneliness or social isolation. Sometimes referred to as "coping groups," they provide support for group members and provide an opportunity to learn how others have coped with similar problems. Most self-help groups feature a fellowship network, including telephone as well as face-to-face contacts between members when other sources of help are not available.

There is a wide array of self-help groups to meet a variety of needs. One that has gained in importance is Widowed Persons Service (WPS) to respond to the problems of persons and provide support, education and social life for their members. A study of widows by Elizabeth Bankhoff (1981) suggests that self-help groups provide a valuable service in several respects: (1) they provide a social network that facilitates adjustment to a changed situation; (2) help members cope with the long-range problems of transition that are usually not available from professionals; and (3) widowed persons rely on other persons who are in a similar life situation for emotional support as they move through the transitional phase.

Other self-help groups are designed to meet the needs of family members of an older person who is mentally impaired and in long-term care such as the Alzheimer's Disease and Related Disorders Association (ADRDA) which has developed across the nation in response to the needs of Alzheimer patients and their families. The association carries on a public education program and awareness campaign to destroy the myth that "senility" is an inevitable and natural part of the aging process. The group has chapters in most cities that offer counseling and support to families who are overburdened by the many problems that are associated with caring for an Alzheimer's patient.

These groups are only two among many that can be valuable resources by professionals, by family members, and by older persons themselves.

The helping activities that are provided by most self-help groups include the following: (1) **mutual affirmation**—assuring one another that they are important and worthy persons; (2) **explanation**—a better understanding of one's self or reactions to a given situation; (3) **empathy**—demonstrating an interest in the individual's problem and responding with empathy. An important function of self-help groups is morale building. Group members are often able to assure other members that problems can be worked out; sharing past experiences, thoughts and feelings is also helpful. Self-disclosure, the ability to relate personal thoughts, are also important factors in self-help groups. Most groups also place a high value on positive reinforcement or applauding behavior of their members to recognize their progress.

Reality Orientation and Sensory Awareness. These groups are used in adult day care and institutional settings to improve the level of patients' functioning. Sensory awareness is usually an adjunct to reality orientation. (Reality orientation is described in Chapter 8.)

Remotivation and Resocialization. These forms of group therapy usually follow reality orientation and are used to help patients who are unresponsive, have memory loss and other problems. (Remotivation therapy is described in Chapter 8.)

Creative Expression Groups. Music and dance movement has been employed to engage older persons in creative expression, socialization and personal enhancement (see Chapter 8).

Summary

Group approaches to helping older persons have been useful in various settings and are beneficial in improving socialization skills and creating opportunities for social interaction with others. Because older persons tend to become isolated, group approaches have been instituted by nursing homes, mental hospitals and senior-citizen centers. In addition, the group experience provides emotional support as members learn to deal with the problems of aging with the help of a leader who is empathetic and sensitive to their concerns. Group participants also gain support from one another as they begin to form meaningful relationships in the process of working with one another. The sense of cohesiveness that develops in groups may be the only positive social identification that some older persons maintain, especially those who are residents in a long-term care facility. In such cases, the group is a vehicle for older persons to establish friendships that would not otherwise develop.

Chapter 8

LONG-TERM CARE FOR OLDER PERSONS

Families of older persons are often confronted with a crucial question: "When should an elderly parent or spouse be placed in a long-term care facility?" This question can never be answered in simple terms, because each case must be considered individually. Some older persons may be experiencing mild or recent mental or physical health problems, while others have had severe deficits and impairments over a long period of time. Deciding on an appropriate long-term care plan must therefore be highly individualized and take into account the medical, functional, personal and social factors in making an assessment of the older person's needs.

Several instruments have been developed to make assessments, but the decision about long-term care must take into account the wishes of the individual and family members. The older person should be involved in thinking about possible plans and should be included in the family's discussion when decisions are made. Some families assume that an older person is not capable of deciding what is needed and forget that older persons are entitled to make their own plans about their lives. Some families misinform older persons about institutional care. Such deceptions are always discovered and make older persons feel that they are worthless objects who have no part in controlling their lives.

When families are considering long-term care, the elderly person is often extremely anxious and fearful. Feelings of being abandoned and rejected begin to surface. Adult children and other family members also have strong emotional reactions to placement of an older person. As Brody points out, even under the best of circumstances, the family undergoes severe emotional stress.

> In our culture, another layer is added to the stress experienced even by "normal" families. There still exists strong, deeply internalized, guilt-inducing injunctions against placing an elderly spouse or parent regardless of the most reality-based determinants of that placement. (P. 115.)

The widespread notion that families dump old people into nursing homes or other institutions is not borne out by the facts. Research studies show that the placement of an elderly relative is the last, rather than the first, resort and is considered only after all other alternatives have been exhausted (Brody, p. 96).

Relocation Problems

In recent years, there has been much discussion of the "transplantation shock" that occurs soon after an elderly person is admitted to a long-term care facility. Removal of older persons from their familiar surroundings does indeed have emotional consequences for them and for their families. However, measures can be taken to make the transition to long-term care less painful. If the older person has participated to the fullest extent in making choices, the negative effects of moving are significantly reduced. Studies also indicate that the quality of the environment into which older persons are moved may be a determining factor. Negative impact occurs when the environment is cold and dehumanizing. When older persons are moved to a positive environment that provides a high degree of personal autonomy, respect, concern and affection and opportunities for constructive activity and social interaction, they show marked improvement (Marlowe, 1973).

A crucial factor in a successful adjustment to placement in a long-term care facility is a sense of autonomy and control of one's own destiny. If this factor is absent, residents develop into totally dependent persons; they begin to surrender their lives to the control of others and lose their self-esteem. Other factors that contribute to deterioration in mental health of older persons in long-term care are: loss of occupation and opportunities to use one's time constructively, loss of privacy, identity, lack of freedom, desexualization and infantilization, and loneliness. A positive attitude of the facilities' staff is a significant factor in successful adjustment and helps reduce the negative impact of relocation. Permissive, friendly staff attitudes and positive expectations preserve the residents' dignity and self-respect.

An overprotective staff can infantilize and humiliate residents by depriving them of adult rights or discouraging attempts to remain independent, as Brody suggests:

Too often, the "good" resident is the one who doesn't assert himself. The regressed, brain-damaged individual, incontinent, confused and disoriented may be treated as a child rather than a dignified adult. It is often easier to "do for" than to encourage the resident to do for himself, simpler to use hospital clothes than the resident's own clothes, easier to keep him quiescent through drug "therapy" than to initiate programs of stimulation and activities. (P. 147.)

Therapeutic Programs

Older persons who need long-term care can often benefit from special group programs that improve their morale and social functioning. Among these various programs are: reality orientation, remotivation therapy and milieu therapy.

Reality Orientation. Reality orientation helps alleviate memory deterioration through continual mental stimulation and orientation activities. It is a treatment model that usually occurs in a group setting but may also be carried out on a one-to-one basis. Clients who benefit from RO include older persons who have long-standing histories of mental illness such as depression, bipolar disorders or paranoia. Older persons who are confused gain independence that enables them to function with minimum assistance and care.

Day-care centers use RO principles as a part of an overall therapeutic approach to maintain older persons' functioning so they can remain in the community or live with their families. Various props are used. A calendar keeps clients aware of the date by posting numbers and months on large cardboard spaces. Name tags on three-by-five cards with large print are worn by clients and staff. A schedule for each day is carefully followed. Group members are queried as to the date, time, weather and other facts. New clients who cannot remember this information often poke fun at their own memory loss and soon begin to perform the RO exercises with the help of other group members. Orientation is sometimes maintained by having clients attend the RO sessions at least two days a week, and some may attend up to four days a week if they are experiencing unusual emotional stress.

Orientation may include instruction in grooming, exercise sessions and sing-alongs. Small group classroom sessions, 30 minutes in length, are used to make patients better oriented to time, date, month or the next meal. Simple memory games are employed to stimulate recall ability.

The application of RO has brought about significant changes in institutional care, as Lucille Taulbee (1984) reports:

> After we began the reality orientation program and group classroom sessions, we observed dramatic changes in residents and also in the atmosphere on the unit. Not only were patients more alert and beginning to take care of themselves, but the staff attitude changed. Staff members began to report progress in individual patients and to take pride in their accomplishments. Residents were given verbal reinforcement for success, and failures were given little consideration. (P. 180.)

RO is not a panacea, but when combined with an overall approach that includes other therapies and techniques, it can promote self-esteem and bring about improved social functioning.

Remotivational Therapy. Remotivation therapy is a group technique for stimulating and revitalizing older persons who are no longer interested or involved in the present or the future. The goal of remotivation therapy is to stimulate older persons to become involved in thinking about the real world and to keep them relating to other persons in their environment. Small groups of five to twelve persons meet weekly for a period of three or four months. A group leader who has been trained in the technique of remotivation prepares for each meeting by gathering material on a particular topic. The material relates to something that has meaning for the group members, such as a trip to the seashore or shopping for groceries. Other possibilities are vacations, gardens, sports, rocks, pets, art or holidays.

The group sessions follow a structure that consists of five stages: creating a climate of acceptance; building a bridge to reality through the introduction of the topic; detailed discussion of the subject using the visual aids; involving the group members in talking about work they used to perform; and a summary by the group leader. The leader plans topics that focus on non-pathological interests and behavior. Discussion centers on things that constitute the real world and to which the group members can relate. Topics that deal with individuals' problems are avoided. Older persons can be helped through remotivation therapy by sharing experiences from the past and talking about their former roles.

Remotivation is a therapeutic technique that offers an opportunity for older persons to increase their sense of reality, practice healthy roles and improve their self-image. Most residents in long-term care respond well to RT and become more alert and interested in life. Moody, Baron and

Monk (1970) advocate that a variety of sensory stimuli and forms of social interaction be employed to maintain contact with reality.

Remotivation therapy creates a bridge between the older person and other people's perception of him. Identifying and asserting experience through interaction strengthens the concept of reality. R. S. Garber (1965) points out the objectives of RT:

> Remotivation is based on reality. A goal of the mental health professional is to help mentally-ill persons recognize the realities we recognize.... A patient has sick and healthy roles. Remotivation tells a patient that he is accepted as an individual... with specific features, with many roles, with unique traits that make him distinguishable from everyone else.

Milieu Approaches. Milieu therapy is one of the earliest treatment approaches for working with mentally ill and emotionally disturbed persons in institutional settings and has been aimed at patients of all ages, including the elderly. Milieu therapy is based on the concept that the social environment itself is a form of treatment that can help people who are depressed and withdrawn. Every aspect of the treatment environment is aimed at encouraging individuals to try new skills and respond to positive relationships with staff members. A variety of activities are used in conjunction with milieu therapy: crafts, occupational therapy, music and art therapy and social group experiences. The programs may also include sheltered workshops or involvement in activities outside the hospital.

Milieu therapy requires the full cooperation of all staff members. Everyone in the resident's "people environment" must communicate attitudes of respect and concern at all times. Group activities should offer a wide range of possibilities so that elderly people can choose what they want rather than being pressured into one particular activity. Staff members can develop a program that is suited to meet the special needs and interests of each individual resident. Patients are also assured the right to not participate. Giving residents a choice supports self-respect. Older persons often lose freedom of choice. When denied this freedom, they lose a sense of dignity and self-esteem.

Older people appear to be quite sensitive to their physical surroundings, and those who are in long-term care facilities are more vulnerable than older people in general. Unfortunately, some long-term facilities are not well designed to provide a pleasant and stimulating environment. Improvements can be made with the right use of color, arrangement of furniture to provide privacy; pleasant places where residents can entertain their visitors can provide a more homelike atmosphere and reduce the impersonal institutional look.

Most research reports suggest that milieu therapy is successful in improving behavior and increasing discharge rates in mental hospitals (Gottesman, 1969). Because milieu therapy involves the use of a wide variety of treatment factors, it is difficult to determine which of these account for the change that occurs, but there is little doubt that milieu therapy has been a positive influence in reshaping and improving treatment of patients in many psychiatric hospitals and long-term institutional settings.

Hospice Care

For persons who are facing the reality of an incurable illness, the prospect of long-term care in a hospital or nursing home presents a bleak future. Older persons often fear the prospect of dying alone, without anyone present to help make the end of life less traumatic and with no one near to soothe the pain.

The hospice movement has developed out of a concern about the inhumane and impersonal atmosphere that too often surrounds people who are terminally ill, undergoing both physical pain and emotional suffering. The basic concept of hospice has been well-summarized by Elizabeth McNulty and Robert Holderby (1983) in their book, **Hospice: A Caring Challenge:**

> Today's hospice is a way station for sojourners who are making their final journey. Its philosophy reflects the holistic concern for easing the physical, emotional and spiritual pain of the terminally ill person and for sustaining members of his family. The spreading hospice movement represents a rebirth of the caring concern for persons who are sick and dying—a movement dedicated to help the patient live at the same time he is dying. It represents a change of focus from curing to caring. (P. 3.)

The principles and values that underlie hospice care are aimed at improving the quality of life for the dying person and to sustain the patient's family members' ability to cope with the patient's terminal illness. The values of hospice include the following:

- A high regard for the recipient of care
- Acceptance of death as a natural part of living

- Consideration of the entire family unit as the patient
- Sustaining the patient at home as long as possible
- Helping the patient assume control over his own life
- Teaching the patient self-care
- Reduction or removal of pain and other distressing symptoms
- Comprehensive services by an interdisciplinary team
- Continuity of services after death

In contrast to other forms of long-term care, hospice places emphasis on care of the patient rather than curing the disease. The hospice concept is not a technical skill designed to eradicate or treat a diagnosed illness. Rather, it is a way to provide a caring environment without representing false hopes of a recovery from a serious sickness. Therefore, hospice care emphasizes relief of symptoms when restoration of health is no longer possible.

Control of symptoms is a basic goal of hospice care. Pain, or the fear of pain, is an all-consuming concern of dying persons. Relief from pain is one of the basic components of hospice care. Being relieved of pain makes the person feel safe and permits him to turn his attention and energies to matters other than his suffering. The relief of pain includes the use of drugs that are effective but are not either sedative or euphoric. A number of preparations that prevent pain, erase the memory of pain and keep the patient alert are available. Brompton's Mixture containing morphine sulfate and a flavoring such as grenadine syrup is now commonly used in the United States and is easy to administer.

Although relief from pain is an important goal of hospice care, there are other aspects of the program that have proven to be highly beneficial to patients and their families. Hospice care extends beyond the walls of a hospital. A full repertoire of services includes home care, day and night care and bereavement services. Home health services provide care for patients in their own homes and allow the person to remain in familiar surroundings. Remaining at home increases the patient's control over his own life, permits him to make choices and decisions, and enhances his feelings of independence and self-sufficiency. Staff members may make daily visits when symptom control is a problem or when the family needs more emotional support. When the person dies at home, a staff member is assigned to act as bereavement counselor and may maintain contact with the family for as long as a year after the patient's death.

Day care or night care are also available in a comprehensive hospice program. Family members may be temporarily relieved of their caretaking responsibilities during the day and the patient returns home for the night. Patients can remain with their families for part of a day or night. Hospice services complement home care and provide respite for family members who often undergo periods of stress. The flexibility in providing this type of inpatient care enables the program to meet the needs of the patient and the family on an individual basis.

There is increasing interest in the development of hospice programs throughout the United States. Community groups have begun to develop independent or hospital-affiliated hospice services. Nursing homes are beginning to add hospice wings or units. Large urban hospitals may have a hospice unit that differs from acute services. The hospice unit looks different; the environment is homelike and non-institutional. The policy and procedure is likely to be less rigid in the hospice unit. Visiting hours are relaxed so that families can spend as much time as possible with the patient. The pace of the hospice unit is slower than in other units because there are few rigid routines of tests and checks that must be followed.

There is little doubt that the hospice movement, although relatively new in the United States, has had a significant impact on health care:

> Hospice has intruded into the spiral of health care technology with startling impact. It has not been the newness of hospice, but rather its challenge to the humanness of health care that has disturbed the status quo. Hospice has advocated for the quality of life, for living until death, for the absence of pain, for the maintenance of personal control, for the maintenance of the family. Hospice is being folded into a larger philosophical framework in which there is renewed recognition that emotional well-being is as important as physical health. (Koff, 1980, p. 172.)

Community Mental Health

Unfortunately, older persons do not receive effective help for psychological problems because they are believed to be incapable of responding to therapy. Professional mental health workers often feel that their efforts would be wasted on the elderly and turn their attention to younger persons they believe would benefit from therapy. This pessimistic attitude is not easily overcome, because ageism has been institutionalized in American culture. However, it is also unjustified. Even seemingly intractable problems can be dealt with if older persons are offered an opportunity to obtain the necessary psychiatric and social services. If denied such help, many will rapidly deteriorate and eventually become chronic patients in nursing homes or mental hospitals.

Once older persons are relegated to custodial care, several consequences follow. First, there is the difficult problem of relocating the person from familiar surroundings which, in itself, is very stressful and increases the risk of mortality. Second, institutional care encourages excessive dependence and surrounds older persons with an environment that results in physical and mental deterioration. Staff members take over many activities that the individual can perform for himself, decreasing their confidence in their ability to function normally. As a consequence, some patients lose functions and abilities that they had before they entered the institution. The effects of institutionalization have been described by Lieberman (1969) as including "poor adjustment, depression and unhappiness, intellectual ineffectiveness, negative self-image, feelings of personal insignificance and impotency, and a view of the self as old. Residents tend to be docile, submissive, show a low range of interests and activities and live in the past, rather than the future. They are withdrawn and unresponsive in relation to others" (p. 331).

Attention has recently been focused on alternative programs that keep older persons in the community where they can receive outpatient care. The overriding goal is to support those areas of independent functioning that the person retains despite some degree of physical and mental disability through a comprehensive community mental health plan. A community treatment plan includes three dimensions: (1) housing services for the physical maintenance of the individual; (2) clinical services to treat psychiatric problems; and (3) life-enhancing and prevention services.

Accommodation services include communal housing, congregate housing, halfway houses, board and care facilities, intermediate care and skilled-care nursing homes.

Clinical services consist of therapeutic day-care programs, general hospital psychiatric wards, community mental health clinics and other outpatient mental health services.

Preventive, supportive and life-enhancing programs include nutrition programs, social daytime programs, peer support groups, adult education programs and transportation services.

Underlying the community mental health movement is the principle of "minimum intervention." It is differentiated from intervention that causes people to be removed from familiar surroundings and be placed in an institution. To implement minimum intervention, mental health personnel take into account what is least disruptive to the individual and focus attention on maintaining a comfortable environment in which the older person feels secure. Mental health personnel work with the client's family in order to prevent unnecessary institutionalization. If an individual manifests some eccentricities, it is not in itself an indication of the need for custodial care. A careful assessment should be made and alternative plans should be considered before a final decision is made to admit the older person to a hospital or nursing home.

Coordination of services is the key to an effective community-care program, especially in cases that require careful follow-up of patients discharged from a psychiatric facility. Patients are likely to encounter many adjustment problems when they return to the community, and unless supportive services are available, they will suffer another serious psychiatric episode that requires re-admission to the hospital. The problems inherent in designing a coordinated community-care program are not easily overcome, but unless they are dealt with effectively many clients will "fall between the cracks." Referral of the clients from one agency to another can result in a series of frustrating experiences that cause older persons to give up in despair. To prevent this, the professional must often take direct responsibility for ensuring that clients receive the services to which they are entitled. Many problems of older persons go beyond the usual psychotherapeutic process. A client who is depressed may be facing serious financial deprivation but is not aware of eligibility for SSI payments. In such cases, the psychotherapist can act in behalf of the client in order to meet an urgent need. A social worker who is involved in assisting an older person work out an appropriate low-cost housing plan may also engage the client in other areas of concern. By planned and skillful intervention on several levels of service, older clients will not be shuffled from one person to another, and a professional relationship of trust can be established to help them live in the community and prevent unnecessary institutionalization of many of our senior citizens.

Finally, the various services that the community provides should be considered in developing a treatment plan. If a health problem needs attention, there needs to be ample facilities to which the client can turn. If there are financial problems, the client needs to be referred to the appropriate sources of help. Usually, a variety of social services are needed, and the presence of a strong network of professional social workers is an invaluable aid to older clients trying to cope with a wide range of problems. Whenever possible, social workers who specialize in working with older persons should be included in the assessment process and actively engaged in formulating the projected treatment plan.

Chapter 9

COPING WITH DYING AND DEATH

Terminal illness is a trying experience for dying patients and their families. It is also a difficult time for health care professionals who are aware that medical intervention cannot restore the patient's health or prevent death. Because the emotions that accompany dying are so intense, doctors, nurses, social workers, hospital aides and administrators need to have a sympathetic understanding of the meaning of dying and an appreciation of the importance of preparing patients and their families for the ending of life.

Fear of Death

Society has shrouded death in mystery and created a conspiracy of silence that makes the acceptance of dying extremely difficult. So pervasive is the need to ignore death that neither professional caretakers or family members are usually willing to admit that the patient is going to die. This conspiracy of silence cuts off honest communication between patients and important persons in their environment. Unable to share their fears about dying, terminally ill patients become emotionally isolated and are unwittingly rejected by those who are in a position to help them overcome their fears.

People fear death for several reasons. The possibility of extreme pain and suffering make dying a frightening experience for many older persons. Indeed, there are many distressing symptoms during a terminal illness. Persistent and severe pain, sleeplessness, loss of bladder and bowel control, nausea, loss of appetite, difficulty in breathing and other forms of physical discomfort are to be expected. But wise use of drugs can control most of these symptoms. Suffering can be eliminated in most cases and can be effectively reduced in all cases. The idea of "death agony" is not an accurate description of dying, because physicians have a wide choice of drugs that are quite effective in controlling pain.

Some people fear dying because it means losing control of their lives.

Many older persons are afraid that when they become sick they will be unable to care for themselves and must depend on others to bathe, dress and feed them. For those who place a high value on being independent, becoming a burden on others is a matter of great concern and they often actively resist taking help from others.

Fear of being abandoned and isolated is also associated with dying. Terminal illness usually brings about a state of helplessness and dependency that creates a great deal of anxiety for many patients. The possibility that a nurse, a doctor or a family member might not be available in time of need is indeed a very disturbing thought.

A loss of self-image is also associated with dying. Marked changes in appearance, loss of sexual attractiveness and inability to function normally contribute to negative attitudes toward death. For those who have led active, vigorous lives, and those who have placed a high value on their physical fitness or attractiveness, death is a very strong threat to the ego.

For most people, death is an ending that leaves many things undone, words not spoken, wishes unfulfilled, tasks to be finished, dreams to be realized. Lack of time to reach a certain goal, to complete a task may become a major barrier to the acceptance of death for some people. Those who can look back on their life span with a sense of "having lived a good life and having run a good race" will have less difficulty accepting death. Rather than being engulfed in a state of despair, they will have achieved a feeling of what Erickson has called "integrity"—a sense of satisfaction in having contributed something of value during one's lifetime.

Death also represents a separation from other valued persons: friends, sons, daughters, husbands or wives. For some, there is much concern about the well-being of those who survive. A dying husband may fear that a wife who has depended on him for support and companionship will not be able to care for herself without his help. Death also has a significant effect on the emotional well-being of the surviving mate. A sense of loneliness, a feeling of being incomplete, and the fear of living out one's life without a partner is often devastating.

The fear of death involves both the dying patient and the family, especially in case of long-term illness. Every member of the family is affected from the very outset, and grieving may take place before death finally occurs. The prospective loss of one who has meant much over a lifetime is disruptive to the lives of family members. Therefore, attention must be given to the family's need for support and understanding during the terminal illness. Mental health professionals can help the family through this period of bereavement, provide comfort, recognize their sorrow, and enable them to begin life anew with a more profound understanding of the meaning of death.

Emotional Responses To Dying

Kubler-Ross, a psychiatrist who interviewed over two hundred dying patients, found that almost all passed through five fairly distinct stages during a terminal illness: denial, anger, bargaining, depression and acceptance. Each individual uses these defenses in a unique way. Some deny that they will die until the very end of life. Others are willing to accept their fate after a relatively brief period of denial. Anger, rage and resentment may not be openly expressed by some patients, while others become overtly hostile. A feeling of sadness is universal among dying persons, but the depth of despair varies and the duration of depression also differs from patient to patient. Most patients eventually accept the inevitability of their death. With time and help from family, friends and professional caretakers, they gradually reach a stage when they are neither depressed nor angry. This is the stage of acceptance.

Denial and Isolation

When patients first learn about the terminal nature of their illness, they almost always respond, "No. It can't be true. I can't really be dying." Some go to great lengths to prove that a mistake has been made and seek support for their denial. They may insist that x-rays have been "mixed up" or that laboratory tests were not really conclusive. If this attempt does not validate their denial, patients may look for another physician who will confirm their belief that a wrong diagnosis was made even though they are partially aware that the original diagnosis was correct. In some cases, patients recognize that they are quite ill, but they reject the threat of death by placing a more comfortable interpretation on their situation. Patients may say: "They brought me in here because I need a rest. I've just been trying to do too much."

Some patients act as though they are going to survive even though they have been told about the life-threatening nature of their illness. They may refuse to accept treatment or ignore the doctor's orders. Studies indicate that as many as one out of five patients not only deny that they have cancer, they insist that they have never been told about the nature of their illness even though they have actually been informed that their situation is extremely serious.

Anger

Feelings of anger, rage and resentment begin to emerge when patients can no longer deny that they are dying. They begin to ask themselves: "Why me?" "This is so unfair." "What did I do to deserve this?" The patient's anger is spent on all or any people around him. Nothing seems to please. Patients complain that they are neglected, that doctors are unavailable, and that they are not receiving proper care. Hostile behavior is also a bid for attention as well as an outlet for anger. It is as if the patient is saying: "I'm still alive and don't you forget it." Most patients will reduce their angry demands if they are given respect and attention despite their obnoxious behavior and are seen as valued human beings. If they know that they do not need to throw a temper tantrum to be listened to or that a nurse will look in on them without having to ring the bell, the patient's temper tantrums will gradually diminish.

Being tolerant of a patient's rational or irrational anger is not easy to achieve. You can easily become upset, because it is unfair for patients to be difficult when you are trying to help them. Most of the anger, you must remind yourself, is directed toward other persons, and you are simply a lightening rod that attracts the hostility at the moment. It may be some comfort to know that expressing anger will usually bring some sense of relief to the dying patient. It also helps if you know that, given the same situation, you might be just as angry as your patients.

Bargaining

Bargaining is sometimes used by dying persons for a brief period in an attempt to postpone the inevitable. Some patients believe that there is a possibility that they will be granted a "second chance" and get a reprieve from death. Most bargains are made with God and are usually kept secret. Patients may use bargaining in an attempt to resolve guilt about an event that occurred in their earlier life and the hope that they will be forgiven for past acts that were injurious to others. It is as though these patients are saying: "I'll be good if only you will let me live," and in most cases the "promises" are meant to stave off the consequences of what is seen as wrongful behavior.

Depression

When patients realize that they cannot postpone dying, they go through a period of depression. Patients feel they are in the process of losing everything and everybody they loved and gave them an incentive to live. Kubler-Ross refers to this period as "preparatory grief" when patients are gradually beginning to accept their death. At this point, encouragement and reassurance are not helpful to patients; for the most part, a period of silent understanding is more meaningful than attempts to cheer patients up and hope that they will not remain sad and depressed. "The patient should not be encouraged to look at the sunny side of things," says Kubler-Ross (1969), "as this would mean he should not contemplate his impending death. It would be contraindicated to tell him not to be sad. . . . If he is allowed to express his sorrow he will find a final acceptance much easier, and he will be grateful to those who sit with him during this stage without telling him not to be sad" (p. 87).

A depression stage is usually difficult for family members. They do not want to see their loved one in a state of profound sadness, but attempts to cheer him up only make dying more difficult because it interferes with the patient's efforts to prepare himself for the end of his life. In working with the patient's family, it is important to help them understand that depression is necessary and enables the patient to move on to an acceptance of death and achieve a sense of inner peace. Family members need to be aware that there is little need for words at this point. A touch of the hand, a stroking of the hair, or just sitting together in silence is the most effective way for family members to express their understanding and support.

Acceptance

After patients have had a sufficient time to mourn their impending loss, they are ready to move to the stage of acceptance and can begin to contemplate the ending of their lives with a certain degree of quiet expectation. This is a period during which patients do not express strong feelings. Much of their time may be spent in sleeping and they will often doze off in brief intervals. Some patients do not welcome visitors, because they are not in a talkative mood and prefer short visits. Patients do want to know that they have not been forgotten. They want to know that someone cares, but the communication usually takes a non-verbal form, as Kubler-Ross points out:

The patient may just make a gesture for us to sit down for a while. He may just hold our hand and ask us to sit in silence. Such moments of silence may be the most meaningful communications for people who are not uncomfortable in the presence of a dying person.... We may just let him know that it is alright to say nothing when the important things are taken care of and it is only a question of time when he can close his eyes forever. It may reassure him that he is not left alone when he is no longer talking and a pressure of the hand, a look, a leaning back in the pillow may say more than many "noisy" words. (P. 113.)

In the acceptance stage, patients gradually detach themselves from their environment, even from their relationship to persons who have been meaningful in their lives. This state of detachment and withdrawal almost always disturbs family members. It is difficult for them to understand that someone they love is willing to die. Stewart Alsop, who wrote about his own experience with cancer, said: "A dying man needs to die, as a sleepy man needs to sleep, and there comes a time when it is wrong, as well as useless, to resist."

Helping Patients Cope With Dying

We live in a culture that is "death denying." It is not surprising that doctors, nurses and other hospital personnel have difficulty in dealing with patients who face inevitable death. We avoid talking with dying patients and fail to give them an honest opinion based on the assumption that the truth would only inflict more pain and mental anguish.

However, surveys indicate that the overwhelming majority of terminally ill patients do want to know if a diagnosis indicates that they have an incurable disease. When 560 patients seen in a tumor clinic were asked if they wanted to know if their illness was fatal, 80 percent said they did want to know. Only 12 percent said they did not. Patients said that they wanted to know the truth because it helped them understand what was happening to them, could settle their affairs and have peace of mind (Simpson, p. 92).

Yet, most doctors do not think it is wise to tell their patients the truth about a terminal illness. Some 80 to 90 percent never, or very seldom, give patients a totally honest answer. When they are asked if their illness is incurable, or want an answer to a direct question, "Is it cancer?" the physician is often evasive. It appears that many doctors and nurses are more frightened of death than the general public. A refusal to talk about death to their patients is often due to the hospital personnel's personal problems in facing death or in an inability to admit that medical science cannot always save a person's life. The reassurance that doctors or nurses give their patients is more for their own benefit than for the person who is dying.

Doctors, nurses and other medical personnel who feel uneasy about talking to a terminally ill patient often ask a chaplain or priest to handle the problem. Or, physicians who are unable to see a patient die will give explicit orders that all staff members refrain from talking to patients about dying. Kubler-Ross (1969) points out that doctors who are extremely uncomfortable about dying are unable to help patients through the denial stage when they need to know the truth in order to deal with the end of life. "I am convinced," she says, "from the many patients with whom I have spoken about this matter, that those doctors who need denial themselves will find it in their patients and those who can talk about the terminal illness will find their patients better able to face and acknowledge it" (p. 32).

Patients can be helped to take a positive approach to dying if their caretakers are not afraid to talk about approaching death. Indeed, to speak about accepting death or even preparing for the end of life can be very beneficial, as Cindy Saunders discovered in working with cancer patients. She writes:

> To talk of approaching death when its approach has become inevitable is not mere resignation on the part of the patient nor defeatism or neglect on the part of the doctor. Certainly they will take no steps to hasten its coming, but for both of them it is the very opposite of doing nothing. The patient may well achieve more in this part of his life than in any other, making of it a real reconciliation and fulfillment. (P. 72.)

Patients usually know the truth even if the doctor wants to keep it from them. When doctors and nurses do not talk to patients about the serious nature of their illness and when they are subjected to a variety of complicated medical procedures and no one gives them a convincing explanation of what is happening, most patients conclude that the truth is being kept from them. Patients also have many indirect ways of picking up information about their condition when they do not receive it directly from their doctor.

Patients want to know the truth because it provides an opportunity to talk openly and honestly about dying. The truth need not be forced on patients irrespective of their wishes. But, you will know when a patient is ready to deal with dying. There are clues that patients want to talk, and you can use these "door openers" to engage in a conversation that will produce vastly different results than you anticipate. A patient may be visibly upset at first, but the open expression of feeling will be an important step in helping patients accept dying with equanimity. Lauren Trombley, a young psychiatrist dying of leukemia, showed great insight into the situation dying persons face: "People wrongly assume that a sick person should be protected from strong, particularly negative, feelings. The truth is that there is probably no more crucial time in a person's life when he needs to know what is going on with those who are important to him."

Doctor Avery Weisman points out that patients can find a profound sense of relief once they learn that their illness cannot be cured. He cites the case of an 85-year-old man who was dying of carcinoma. He had not been told about the true nature of his illness. Soon after he learned that he had cancer, he approached his death with dignity and composure. Weisman recalls the event: "Several weeks before he died, the patient's son requested a consultant's opinion about pain medication. During this brief interview, the patient suddenly asked the doctor, "Do I have cancer?" When told that he did, the patient said, "Why didn't someone tell me before now?" He seemed somewhat less troubled during the next few days, and it was surmised that the new pain medication produced better results. Beside relieving the pain, however, the medication evidently improved the patient's spirits. He also ate better, slept well and did not complain about his fear of dying.

One evening, as his daughter made him comfortable before leaving the hospital room, she said good night and told him she would see him in the morning. The old man looked straight at her and slowly shook his head. "Are you afraid?," she asked. He answered with gentleness, "Why, of course I'm afraid," with none of the anguish that had so disturbed him earlier. Then he went to sleep and did not awaken (Weisman, p. 182).

When doctors do not help patients work through their feelings about dying, they become isolated and must face death alone. A dying patient describes the pain of isolation and expressed the hope that doctors will be available to help her confront death:

> I am just the old, hopeless case in the corner bed, forgotten. If I cry out, no one will hear me. I don't expect to be found. No one will look for

me: nobody knows I'm lost.... I believe the fear could be eliminated if the doctor would only talk it over with us. Little by little, we could work with him, to face the end.... Be gentle without being maudlin, care and do so truly. At this stage, there is an uncanny clarity of true and false. Lack of sincerity is so obvious it is cruel. (Simpson, p. 52.)

Dying With Dignity

Older persons should be permitted to die with dignity and composure. Doctor Avery Weisman describes how a 59-year-old widow suffering from cancer that no longer responded to treatment faced death with dignity. In the terminal phase of her illness, she began to reflect on her impending death. "I have lost many loved ones," she said, "but I never saw anyone die. I don't know how to die." She deeply appreciated that her oldest son came to stay at her side during the final days. She dreamed of a resort hotel where she and her husband had vacationed. When she awoke, she asked for a calendar of saints so she could choose a good day to die. Thereafter, she seemed to dwell on her impending death, complaining that God, for His own good reasons, had let her linger so long. Truly, after so much travail, she was facing death with a strong sense of dignity, choice and comportment, traits that had distinguished her life (Weisman, p. 132).

To enable a person to die with dignity, attention must be centered on relieving the patient's discomfort rather than curing the disease. There is no dignity in pain, in incontinence, in nausea or other manageable symptoms. All these symptoms rob patients of their ability to live out their lives with dignity. The chronic pain that accompanies terminal illness is unremitting and must be well-controlled, or better yet, completely eliminated. Rather than withholding painkilling drugs until the patient demands relief, once it is definite that a person is dying, the drugs can be used to prevent the pain from occurring in the first place. If analgesics are given frequently and in large enough dosages, the patient can rest assured that pain will not return. When patients are confident that they will be as pain-free as possible, they will be more at ease because they are always one step ahead of the pain and their anxiety will be sharply reduced.

Providing emotional and psychological support is essential to help patients die with dignity. When the staff is primarily concerned with the progress of the disease, the value and dignity of the patient may be forgotten. Reaffirming and nurturing the patient's sense of individuality and worth can be achieved in many ways. Addressing patients as adults who understand, rather than talking down to them as though they are mentally deficient or children, is very important to maintaining dignity. Performing small favors, washing a patient's hair, helping write a letter, moving the bed closer to the window are ways to bolster the patient's morale. Touch is extremely important: holding hands, caressing the face, and stroking the hair are non-verbal forms of communication that express love and caring to the dying person.

Terminally ill patients must have the right to control their own lives if their dignity is to be preserved. There is little reverence shown to older persons in our society and even less to them when they are dying. But, if the patient's wishes and concerns are respected, if they feel they have some control over their environment and can have their decisions accepted, a sense of personal value and worth will begin to emerge. Staff should convey a message that they are vitally interested in the special needs of each patient, invite requests and respond positively to them. By so doing, they will give concrete evidence that they respect the person's right to control his life. Respecting the individual's life-style, regard for ethnic background, cultural orientation and moral values are important in creating an environment that promotes a sense of self-worth, personal identity and dignity.

The dying person should also be assured that he will not be forgotten or deserted at death. The most frequently expressed fear of dying persons is that they will die alone. Those who have no close relatives or social contacts are especially isolated and fear that no one will soothe their pain or respond to a crisis. Unfortunately, visits from friends become infrequent as patients deteriorate; opportunities to be in touch with important others often lessen as death approaches. Volunteers can provide this much-needed care when friends and family are not available at the ending of life.

Doctor Kubler-Ross comments on what death means to terminally ill persons: "We have learned that for the patient death itself is not the problem, but dying is feared because of the accompanying sense of hopelessness, helplessness and isolation." The need for terminally ill persons to be treated with respect is set forth in the following "Dying Patients' Bill of Rights."

The Dying Patient's Bill of Rights*

- I have the right to be treated as a living human being until I die.
- I have the right to maintain a sense of hopefulness however changing its focus may be.
- I have the right to be cared for by those who can maintain a sense of hopefulness however changing this might be.
- I have the right to express my feelings and emotions about my approaching death in my own way.
- I have the right to participate in decisions concerning my care.
- I have the right to expect continuing medical and nursing attention even though "cure" goals must be changed to "comfort" goals.
- I have the right not to die alone.
- I have the right to be free from pain.
- I have the right to have my questions answered honestly.
- I have the right not to be deceived.
- I have the right to have help from and for my family in accepting my death.
- I have the right to die in peace and dignity.
- I have the right to retain my individuality and not be judged for my decisions which may be contrary to beliefs of others.
- I have the right to discuss and enlarge my religious and/or spiritual experiences, whatever these may mean to others.
- I have the right to expect that the sanctity of the human body will be respected after death.
- I have the right to be cared for by caring, sensitive, knowledgeable people who will attempt to understand my needs and will be able to gain some satisfaction in helping me face my death.

The Right To Die

Should terminally ill patients have the right to die? This is an exceptionally emotional and volatile issue. There is growing sentiment that approves of voluntary euthanasia if the patient so chooses. A Lou Harris

---

*This Bill of Rights was created at a workshop on "The Terminally Ill Patient and the Helping Person," in Lansing, Michigan, sponsored by the Southwestern Michigan Inservice Education Council and conducted by Amelia J. Barbus, Associate Professor of Nursing, Wayne State University, Detroit. From *American Journal of Nursing*, 75 (January 1975): 99. Reprinted with permission.

poll taken in 1977 indicated that 71 percent of Americans believe that a patient with a terminal illness ought to be able to tell his doctor to let him die rather than extend his life when no cure is in sight.

The medical profession faces a serious dilemma when confronted with a patient's wish to die. Doctors take an oath that they will relieve suffering. They also take an oath that they will prolong life. Under present law, they must choose between allowing patients to suffer for a prolonged period or granting their request to die. In practice, physicians find a way to grant a terminally ill patient's request; they do not take extreme measures to prolong life if no foreseeable cure is available. The American Medical Association states that the "cessation of the employment of extraordinary means to prolong life of the body when there is irrefutable evidence that biological death is imminent is the decision of the patient and/or his immediate family" (AMA, 1973).

The family also faces a serious dilemma when confronted with having to give consent to passive euthanasia. Watching a loved family member deteriorate and witnessing the pain of a terminal illness can be a horrible, heart-rending experience. The responsibility for making a life-or-death decision weighs heavily on the minds and hearts of family members. They may well ask themselves what purpose is served by extending life when it no longer has meaning? How long should their loved one endure pain and suffering? While health care workers cannot and should not attempt to make a decision for the family or the patient, they should be available for consultation and professional advice during this very difficult time.

Helping Families Cope With Terminal Illness

Families of terminally ill patients undergo strong emotional reactions to the imminent death of a loved one. At first, the family may deny the reality of the illness, arrange for visits or consultations with other clinics and physicians in an effort to prove that the original diagnosis is not accurate. In many cases, the families will act as though the patient is not seriously ill and carry out a pretense that they think will help but only hinders the patient from making a peaceful transition to death. Encouraging families to honestly communicate with patients and give up these deceitful games can be the first step toward improving the relationship between the patient and the family. If each tries to keep dying secret from the other, open communication will be difficult and there can be no genuine sharing of deep feelings that may go unexpressed.

Family members are often plagued by the thought that they did not do enough to prevent the onset of the illness. Although it may help to assure the family that there was nothing they could have done, it is more helpful to simply listen to what they have to say and help them work through their grief and guilt. Dying patients may also have a wide range of withheld feelings and need an opportunity to express them as they approach death. They often want to look back over their past lives and talk about important events. Such a "life review" is a significant part of dying, says Robert Butler (1975): "In the course of life review, an older person may reveal to his wife, children and other intimates, unknown qualities of his character and unstated actions of his past. In return, they may reveal undisclosed or unknown truths. Hidden themes of great vintage may emerge, changing the quality of a lifelong relationship. Revelations of the past may forge a new intimacy, render a deceit honest; they may sever peculiar bonds and free tongues; or they may sculpture terrifying hatred of fluid, fitful antagonisms" (p. 496).

The most difficult time for the family occurs when the dying person has accepted the inevitable ending of life. During this phase, patients are slowly detaching themselves from their families and want to be visited less frequently. Some prefer to see only one family member during this period, and family members will often feel rejected when they are shut off from a loved person with whom they have had contact over a long lifetime. It is important to help family members understand that this detachment, this separation from valued ties, is a normal and necessary part of dying. Families need a great deal of support at this point in order to avoid serious misinterpretations that can create problems if a careful explanation is not given.

Grief and Mourning

The sorrow that follows the loss of a family member involves profound physical, mental and emotional changes that can inflict serious psychological damaging on the survivors. The most immediate effect is a period of numbness or shock and a general lack of responsiveness that last for about one week after which more acute symptoms of distress appear: depression, sleep disturbances, and frequent crying. Additional symptoms of emotional upheaval include pain attacks, difficulty in thinking, complaints of poor memory, irritability, anger and feelings of guilt. In some cases, the bereaved person may experience hallucinations or develop a variety of somatic problems such as intestinal disorders, difficulty in breathing or extreme exhaustion.

The impact on a surviving spouse, usually the widow, has an enduring effect. A period of intense grief follows the death of the spouse and lasts about one to three months, during which the individual is preoccupied with thoughts about the lost mate and has a compulsion to dwell on the past. There is also a compulsion to retrieve the deceased in some irrational manner. Some individuals may experience hallucinations in which the lost mate is actually present. This period of mourning also involves aimless wandering and restlessness, a feeling that time is suspended and not knowing what to do. Events around them appear to be unreal, and there is a general disorganization in thought and emotion that causes some individuals to fear that they are becoming mentally ill.

Feelings of guilt are common during bereavement. Guilt is associated with circumstances that surrounded the death of the mate. Survivors often say that they should have done more to change the course of the illness. Or, they become angry toward the physician for not having given their mate enough care and attention. In some cases, survivors become angry toward family and friends who they think have abandoned them in their grieving. If the anger cannot be expressed outwardly, it is likely to turn inward and be repressed. Depression, nightmares, psychosomatic disorders and even thoughts of suicide may follow. Depressive symptoms may range from a mild form of blues to a psychotic illness. There is an important distinction between those individuals who go through the grieving process in a normal way and those who fall into a state of depression.

- The bereaved retain the capacity for pleasure; depressives have lost the capacity to have fun.
- The bereaved dwell on that which was lost; depressives dwell on themselves.
- The bereaved may be openly angry; depressives may be irritable, critical, complaining but open anger is missing.
- The bereaved feel the world is empty, but realize that their sense of personal emptiness is temporary; depressives feel a prolonged, intense inner emptiness. (Simos, p. 190.)

Most individuals are able to surmount the depressive feelings that follow a major loss and can begin to rebuild their lives. Indeed, there is a strong psychic push toward restitution in an attempt to restore psychological equilibrium that unites the past and the present. This restitution process comes in the final stage of grieving. It involves two steps: first, actual recognition that the lost person is gone and cannot be retrieved; second, a gradual step-by-step relinquishing of ties to the deceased. The catharsis of grieving lays the groundwork for restitution by helping the survivor integrate the experience of loss, gain a renewed sense of self and form new attachments that give meaning to life.

Counseling bereaved persons can have several benefits. A supportive approach is usually a prime requisite in helping survivors cope with the loneliness and distress that follows the death of a mate. Having a confidant with whom one can share these feelings is an important factor in improving the survivor's morale. Giving information about what the experience means is also helpful. Many survivors think that their reactions to the death of a loved person are abnormal, especially when they feel that the deceased spouse is still actually present. If they are helped to put these experiences into a broad perspective, most survivors will begin to understand that anger, guilt and extreme loneliness are natural and normal reactions as a result of a major loss.

Steps in the Helping Process

Working with dying patients is a difficult and complex undertaking. However, it can be made less difficult if mental health workers have a fairly clear answer to the following questions:

1. What is the goal of treatment in working with terminally ill patients and their families?
2. What is the nature of my relationship to the patient during this crucial period?
3. How can I best carry out my role and responsibilities to patients and their families?
4. How can I prepare myself to carry out these responsibilities?

Goals in Treatment

One of your first responsibilities is to decide what you and your colleagues are attempting to achieve in the helping process. In working with patients who are inevitably going to die because there is no cure for their condition in sight, the goal is to make the ending of life as painless and free of suffering as possible. As Avery Weisman points out, the caregiver's chief obligation is to provide "safe conduct" for the dying patient. To go on pressing for active treatment that aggressively seeks to extend the patient's life is not an appropriate goal. Such measures simply prolong dying and are not necessarily the right or kind choice in determining your treatment goal. Patients become very weary with the pain of dying. When he was dying, Sir William Osler said, "I'm too far across the river now to want to come back and have it all over again." Recognizing that treatment will not restore the patient to health but only prolong pain is not an act of defeatism for the medical personnel or the patient; it shows respect and awareness of the individual and preserves his dignity.

To provide safe conduct for dying patients, your efforts can best be directed toward: (a) freeing the patient from physical pain, (b) assisting the patient cope with the emotional suffering involved in dying, and (c) helping the family cope with the death of a valued person.

Freeing Patients From Pain

Chronic pain is timeless and meaningless, and for many patients the pain is made worse because they anticipate it. Therefore, physicians are becoming aware that it is important to prevent the pain from occurring in the first place rather than trying to control it after it has occurred. Cecily Saunders, who has had wide experience in working with terminally ill cancer patients, points out that pain control can be accomplished without concern about addiction to narcotics:

> The problems of tolerance and dependence can be almost eliminated by the way in which the administration of drugs is managed. It should be part of the whole process of caring for the patient.... If every time the patient has a pain he must ask somebody else for something to relieve it, it reminds him that he is dependent on another person. But if instead, the staff can anticipate the occurrence of pain ... the patient does not continually ask for relief. He can stay alert, thinking of other things and "forgetting" the pain.

Administering drugs is not the only way to relieve pain. Listening to your patients reduces pain and is an effective source of comfort. These lines from a Chinese poem in the ninth century convey the importance of a person-to-person curing relationship: "Tranquil talk was better than any medicine. Gradually the feelings came back to my numbed heart." Informing patients how their medication works, what it is intended to do, is also important. You can assure them that what is being used is effective and that they will be free of pain.

Pain is also a matter that concerns the patient's family. One patient who could think of nothing but her pain said, "I love my family but I couldn't bear to have them in the room because I couldn't think of anything else and they would have seen the pain in my face." When the family knows that careful attention is being given to the control or the elimination of pain, they have an opportunity to turn their attention to other matters of concern to both the patient and themselves.

Relieving Emotional Suffering

The physical pain of dying patients can be relieved by physicians, but their emotional suffering must be dealt with by everyone who is charged with their care. The loss of self-esteem, change in body image, fears of abandonment and isolation, anxiety and feelings of hopelessness must also be treated. To accomplish this goal, clergy, social workers, psychologists, psychiatrists, as well as physicians and nurses use a team approach in which each plays an important role.

Communication among team members is a critical factor in relieving dying patients' emotional suffering. One team member may want to withhold truth about the patient's illness from the family, while others believe that it is unwise to mislead them about the patient's condition. Differences in opinion among staff members can be very confusing to patients and can only add to their anxiety. Communication between the family members will also protect the patient from being exposed to contradictory messages—prevent rifts in the family at a time when unity is essential to help the patient.

Communication between a dying patient and a staff member can provide opportunities for patients to express feelings of depression and grief that they may be reluctant to reveal to family members. However, professional credentials are often less important than a particular person's compassionate response at a time of need. A volunteer may be well-suited for this role. Or a particular family member may be the person who can best help the dying patient cope with the fear of death. If so, these persons should be included as members of the team.

Helping the Family Grieve

This goal is often considered to be outside the realm of professional caretakers and is left to others, especially clergymen. However, studies have shown that grieving occurs before the patient has actually died and that those who take care of the dying patient can be significantly involved in helping the family work through "anticipatory bereavement." Relatives seek answers to many questions: "Why did God let this happen?" "Why did the doctors operate?" "Why didn't I see that he (or she) was ill until it was too late?"

Simply listening is probably the most effective way of helping family members deal with these questions and their feelings of anger and guilt. These expressions of anguish may be more freely expressed to professional staff members or someone who is not a member of the family. If you listen in a sympathetic and non-judgmental way, you will be able to help them cope with their feelings.

In describing how anticipatory grief helps families, Cecily Saunders writes:

> One sees that mourning is not just forgetting. It includes a sense of going back to all the ties and undoing them, and taking out what is really valuable, until in the end what is finally left is no longer grief in the same way, since much has been resolved. This part of the family time together is very important and can make a crucial difference to the whole grieving process.

When it seems as though one patient after another dies, it is very likely that you will wonder how you can help families during this stressful period. Doctor Austin Kutscher suggests that grief can be creative. He writes:

> The grief experience can be transformed into a most meaningful and productive one through emphasis on the concepts and ideals of **creative** grief. The energies expended in grieving can be channeled with enormous productivity into good works or deeds, service to others in distress, or devotion to tasks left undone by the deceased rather than dissipated in unstructured, self-pitying melancholia. (P.21.)

Enabling the families to achieve this state of creative grief is one of the important contributions you can make to turn the death of your dying patients into a renewed spirit that will live on long after their own life has ended.

Learning to Work With the Dying

Most health care professionals are not intellectually or emotionally prepared for death and dying. When they enter this field of practice, they must learn to cope with their reactions to dying patients and have time to work through their feelings about death. Learning to work with terminally ill patients requires a period of adjustment and time to feel comfortable in this helping role. Bernice Harper has developed a paradigm that describes the way in which workers learn to cope with their anxiety and discomfort. Professional competence is achieved over a period of several months during which the worker develops greater confidence in his ability, becomes more aware of his own emotional reactions to dying and gains a high level of satisfaction in helping patients face death. The stages of coping with anxiety in working with the terminally ill is illustrated in Figure 1.

The notes that follow are intended to serve as guidelines for social workers, nurses, hospital aides and other professionals who work with the terminally ill.

Stage 1. *Knowledge and Anxiety*

When you first encounter dying patients, you will discover that you are eager to serve them, but you will also experience some anxiety and emotional discomfort because you are not yet familiar with the problems and needs of your patients. The knowledge that you have already acquired will be helpful. It provides an intellectual basis from which you can begin to operate, and you will rely on intellectualization to guide you in carrying out your role. Much of your energy will be directed toward meeting your patients' tangible requests. You will not yet have the deep and meaningful relation to your patients that comes in later stages of your development. You will tend to work with the patients' family more than with the patients themselves. You will probably not be ready to let the patient talk about death or encourage them to raise sensitive questions that you are not prepared to deal with, because they evoke strong emotions.

180   *Emotional Problems of Aging*

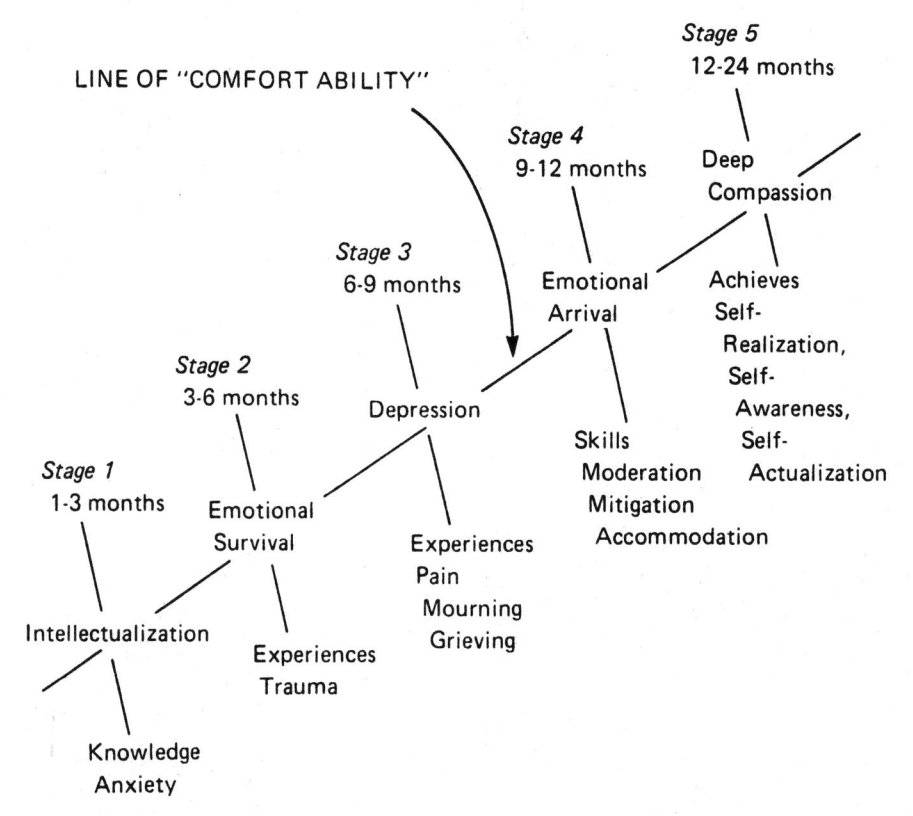

```
                                              Stage 5
                                              12-24 months
        LINE OF "COMFORT ABILITY"                  \
                                    Stage 4        Deep
                                    9-12 months   Compassion
                        Stage 3                \       \
                        6-9 months    Emotional    Achieves
                                \     Arrival      Self-
                                 \       \         Realization,
              Stage 2             \       \        Self-
              3-6 months           \       \       Awareness,
                      \         Depression  \      Self-
    Stage 1            \             \    Skills   Actualization
    1-3 months        Emotional       \  Moderation
          \           Survival         \ Mitigation
           \              \         Experiences Accommodation
            \              \          Pain
   Intellectualization      \        Mourning
         \                   \       Grieving
          \                Experiences
           \                 Trauma
        Knowledge
        Anxiety
```

Figure 1. Coping with Professional Anxiety in Terminal Illness. From Bernice Catherine Harper, *Death: The Coping Mechanism of the Health Professional* (Greenville, South Carolina: Southeastern University Press, 1977). Reprinted with permission.)

Stage 2. *Emotional Survival*

During this stage, you will become more aware of your reactions to dying. The reality of impending death for your patients begins to weigh heavily on your consciousness. You will go through a period of frustration. You realize that you cannot arrest the dying process, but yet you want to fight back in the hope that your patient will survive. You will feel guilty because you are in good health while your patients are deteriorating and becoming helpless. This is also a time when you will begin to confront feelings about your own death and become more emotionally involved with your patients. You will also begin to realize the complexities and magnitude of your task and appreciate the role you play in this area of professional service.

Stage 3. *Depression*

During this stage, you will experience extreme anxiety, grief and depression. You will also have doubts about your usefulness and capability. Your emotional involvement in your work will increase and your relationship to your patients will become more intimate. There will be a tendency for you to become overidentified with your patients and you will mourn for them as your relationship becomes more meaningful and personalized. At this stage, you will also become more aware of your feelings about dying. As you contemplate your own death, you will undergo considerable discomfort. If the frustration and pain are too great or if you do not get adequate rewards from your work, you may decide that you are not well-suited for working with the terminally ill. This is a crucial period. If you can survive the grieving and mourning stage, you can make the transition to the next stage of "emotional arrival" and become a truly valuable professional.

Stage 4. *Emotional Arrival*

At this point, you will begin to become free of the pain and grief that characterized the depression phase of your development. You will feel more comfortable in your relationship to your patients. You will also have more confidence in your ability to help them as you learn to practice your art. You can now accept dying as a natural part of life. The guilt that you once felt will have lessened and you will be better able to cope with your own death anxiety. At this stage, you will develop strong ties with dying patients and their families and be able to act effectively in behalf of the dying patient.

Stage 5. *Deep Compassion*

This stage is characterized by a sense of self-realization and self-fulfillment. It is the culmination of your professional growth. You will be able to accept death and loss, and you will have developed the ability to give of yourself with a feeling that what you do is important and that your profession requires a high degree of knowledge, experience and competence. You will feel that you have been rewarded for your growth and development and take great pride in your ability to work with dying patients.

Summary

When you work with older persons, you will need to be prepared to help them cope with a disabling illness that cannot be cured. Helping others face death is a difficult and demanding task. It requires an understanding of the fears that plague dying people and sound knowledge of what happens to them at various stages of dying. To help those who are entrusted to your care face death, you must eventually come to terms with your own personal feelings about dying in order to talk with them openly and honestly about their denials, anger and sorrow. If the relationship to your patients is characterized by empathy, acceptance and genuineness, they can communicate their anxieties and talk with you about their deepest concerns. Providing safe conduct from life to death is indeed a difficult, often a frustrating task, but it is also one that can be rewarding and satisfying.

REFERENCES

Alarcon, P.R. Hypochondrias and depression in the aged. *Gerontolica Clinica,* 6:266-7, 1964.

Alexander, F.G. The indication for psychoanalytic therapy. *Bulletin of the New York Academy of Medicine,* 20:319-34, 1944.

Allen, E.B., and H.E. Craw. Paranoid reaction in the elderly. *Geriatrics,* 5:66-73, 1950.

Altholz, Judith. Group psychotherapy with the elderly. In: Irene Burnside, *Working with the Elderly.* Belmont, CA: Wadsworth, 1984.

Baldwin, B.A. Crisis intervention in professional practice: Implications for clinical training. *American Journal of Orthopsychiatry,* 47:538-41, 1978.

Baldwin, B.A. A paradigm for the classification of emotional crisis. *American Journal of Orthopsychiatry,* 48:538-51, 1978.

Beck, A.T. et al. An inventory for measuring depression. *Archives of General Psychiatry,* 4:53-63, 1961.

Beck, Aaron. *Cognitive Behavior Therapy and the Emotional Disorders.* New York: International U. Press, 1976.

Bell, J.E. *Family group therapy.* Washington, D.C.: U.S. Government Printing Office, 1961.

Bradford, L., *Retirement.* Chicago, Ill: Nelson-Hall, 1979.

Brody, E., *Long-term Care of Older People.* New York: Human Sciences Press, 1977.

Brecher, E.M. *Love, Sex and Aging.* Boston: Little, Brown, 1984.

Breed, W., and Hafline, C.L. Sex differences in suicide among older White Americans. In O. Kaplan (Ed.), *Psychopathology of Aging.* New York: Academic Press, 1979.

Burgess, A.W., and B.A. Baldwin. *Crisis Intervention Theory and Practice.* Englewood Cliffs, NJ: Prentice-Hall, 1981.

Burgess, E.P. The modification of depressive behaviors. In R.D. Rubin and C.M. Franks (Eds.), *Advances in Behavior Therapy.* New York: Academic Press, 1969.

Busse, E.W. The treatment of hypochondriasis. *Tristate Medical Journal,* 2:7-12, 1954.

Butler, R.N. The life review: an interpretation of reminiscence in the aged. *Psychiatry,* 26:65-76, 1963.

Butler, R.N. *Why Survive: Being Old in America.* New York: Harper & Row, 1975.

Chase, D., *Dying at Home with Hospice.* St. Louis, Mo.: C. V. Mosby, 1986.

Corey, G. *Group: Process and Practice.* Monterey, CA: Brooks-Cole, 1977.

Cormican, E.J. Task-centered model for work with the aged. *Social Casework,* 58:490-94, 1977.

Dengrove, E. Treatment of non-phobic disorders by the behavioral therapies. Lecture to Association for Advancement of the Behavioral Therapies. New York, Dec. 17, 1966.

Ellis, A., *Handbook of Rational Emotive Therapy.* New York; Springer, 1977.

Dollard, J., and N. Miller. *Personality and Psychotherapy.* New York: McGraw-Hill, 1950.

Duke University Center for Study of Aging and Human Development. *Short Portable Mental Status Questionnaire.* Durham, North Carolina: Duke University Press, 1978.

Early, L.W., and O. Von Mering. Growing old the outpatient way. *American Journal of Psychiatry, 125:*963-67, 1969.

Edinberg, M.A. *Mental Health Practice with the Elderly.* Englewood Cliff, NJ: Prentice-Hall, 1985.

Erikson, E. *Childhood and Society.* New York: W. W. Norton, 1963.

Fischer, J., and H. Gochros. *Planned Behavioral Change.* New York: Free Press, 1975.

Frey, P.S. Structured and unstructured reminiscence training and depression among the elderly. *Clinical Gerontologist, I:*15-35, 1983.

Garber, R.S. A psychiatrist's view of remotivation. *Mental Hospitals, 16:*220, 1965.

Garrison, J.E. Stress management training for the elderly. *Journal American Geriatric Society, 26:*397-403, 1978.

Gottesman, L.E. Extended care of the aged: Psychosocial aspects. *Journal Geriatric Psychiatry, 11:*2, 1969.

Haley, J. *Problem-solving therapy.* San Francisco: Jossey-Bass, 1976.

Harris, M.R., B.L. Kales, and E.H. Freeman. Precipitating stress: An approach to brief therapy. *American Journal of Psychotherapy, 17:*465-71, 1963.

Havinghurst, R.J., B.L. Neugarten, and S.S. Tobin. The measurement of life satisfaction. *Journal of Gerontology, 16:*134-43, 1961.

Herr, J., and J. Weakland. *Counseling Elders and Their Families.* New York: Springer, 1979.

Hollis, F. Casework: *A Psychosocial Therapy.* New York: Random House, 1972.

Hussian, R.A. *Geriatric Psychology.* New York: Van Nostrand, Reinhold, 1981.

Kaplan, H.S. *The New Sex Therapy.* New York: Brunner/Mazel, 1974.

Kardener, S.H. A methodological approach to crisis therapy. *American Journal of Psychotherapy, 29:*4-13, 1975.

Kay, D.W., M. Roth, and B. Hopkins. Affective disorders arising in the senium. *Journal of Mental Science, 101:*302-14, 1955.

Koff, T. et al. *Hospice: A Caring Community.* Cambridge, MA: Winthrop, 1980.

Kubler-Ross, E. *On Death and Dying.* New York: Macmillan, 1969.

Kiernet, Jean. The uses of life review activity. In Irene Burnside, *Working With the Elderly.* Belmont, CA: Wadsworth, 1984, p. 300.

Kutner, B. et al. *Five Hundred Over Sixty.* New York: Sage Foundation, 1956.

Lawton, M.P. The functional assessment of elderly people. *Journal American Geriatric Society, 19:*465-481, 1971.

Lazarus, A.A. Learning theory and the treatment of depression. *Behavior Research and Therapy, 6:*83-89, 1968.

Levinson, H. Termination of psychotherapy: Some salient issues. *Social Casework, 59:*588-96, 1977.

Lowenthal, M.J. Some potentialities of a life cycle. In F. Carp (Ed.), *Retirement.* New York: Human Sciences Press, 1972.

Lowy, L. *Social Work With the Aging.* New York: Harper & Row, 1979.

Maddox, G.L. Some correlates of differences in self-assessment of health states among the elderly. *Journal of Gerontology, 17:*180–85, 1962.

Marlowe, R.A. Effects of environment on elderly state hospital relocatees. *Geriatric Focus* 12:31, 1973.

Masters, W. and V. Johnson, *Human Sexual Inadequacy.* Boston, Ma.; Little Brown, 1970.

Matteson, Mary Ann. Group reminiscing for the depressed institutionalized elderly. In: Irene Barnside, *Working With the Elderly.* Belmont, CA: Wadsworth, 1984.

McMahon, A.U., and P.J. Rubideck. Reminiscing. *Archives of General Psychiatry, 19:*292–8, 1964.

McNulty, E., and R. Holdberg. *Hospice: A Caring Challenge.* Springfield, IL: Charles C Thomas, 1983.

Moody, L., K. Baron, and G. Monk. Moving the past into the present. *American Journal of Nursing, 70:*235–36, 1970.

Murphy, G.E., and E. Robbins. The communication of suicide ideas. In H.L. Resnick (Ed.), *Suicidal Behavior.* Boston: Little, Brown, 1968.

O'Leary, K. and G. Wilson, *Behavior Therapy.* Englewood Cliffs, N.J.: Prentice Hall, 1975.

Poggi, R. A psychiatrist's perspective. In Irene Burnside, *Working With the Elderly.* Belmont, CA: Wadsworth, 1984, p. 363.

Parad, H.J. (Ed.). *Crisis Intervention: Selected Readings.* New York: FSAA, 1965.

Peck, R. "Psychological developments in the second half of life." In Neugarten, B. (Ed.), *Middle Age and Aging.* Chicago: University of Chicago Press, 1968.

Perlman, H.H. *Social Casework: A Problem-Solving Process.* Chicago: University of Chicago Press, 1957.

Perlman, H.H. The problem-solving model in social casework. In: Roberts, R. and Nee, R. (Eds.), *Theories of Social Casework.* Chicago: University of Chicago Press, 1970.

Perls, F. *In and Out of the Garbage Pail.* Moab, Utah: Real People, 1969.

Pfeiffer, E. Psychological developments in the second half of life. In Birren, J.E., and K.W. Schail (Eds.), *Handbook of Psychology and Aging.* New York: Van Nostrand, Reinhold, 1977.

Pfeiffer, E. Psychopathology and social psychology. In Birren, J.E. and K.W. Schail (Eds.), *Handbook of Psychology and Aging.* New York: Van Nostrand, Reinhold, 1977.

Post, F. *Persistent Persecutory States in the Elderly.* New York: Pergamon, 1966.

Post, F. *The Significance of Affective Symptoms in Old Age.* London: Oxford, 1962.

Rapoport, L. Crisis intervention as a mode of brief treatment. In Roberts and Nee (Eds.), *Theories of Social Casework.* Chicago: University of Chicago Press, 1970, pp. 267–311.

Reid, W.J., and L. Epstein. *Task-Centered Casework.* New York: Columbia University Press, 1972.

Rogers, C.R. *Client-Centered Therapy.* Boston: Houghton Mifflin, 1951.

Ryden, M. Nursing intervention in support of reminiscence. *Journal of Gerontological Nursing,* 1:461–463, 1981.

Satir, V. *Conjoint Family Therapy.* Palo Alto: Science and Behavior Books, 1964.

Saul, S. *Aging—An Album of People Growing Old.* New York: Wiley, 1974, pp. 20–26.

Schaie, K.W. Age changes in adult intelligence. In D.S. Woodruff and J.E. Birren (Eds.), *Aging, Scientific Perspectives and Social Issues.* New York: Van Nostrand, Reinhold, 1975.

Sherman, E. *Counseling the Aging: An Integrative Approach.* New York: Free Press, 1981.

Simos, B., *A Time to Grieve.* New York: Family Service Association, 1979.

Simpson, M., *Dying, Death and Grief.* New York; Plenum Press, 1979.

Starr, B.D., and Weiner. *The Starr-Weiner Report on Sex and Sexuality in the Mature Years.* New York: Stein and Day, 1981.

Streib, G., *Retirement in American Society.* Ithica, N. Y.: Cornell U., 1971.

Taulbee, L. Reality orientation and clinical practice. In I. Burnside, *Working With the Elderly.* Belmont, CA: Wadsworth, 1984.

Tibbetts, C. *Handbook of Social Gerontology.* Chicago, Il.: University of Chicago Press, 1959.

Tobin, S.S. Psychological factors that influence the safety of the elderly. *Occupational Health Nursing,* 11–12, Feb. 1971.

Turner, F. *Psychosocial Therapy.* New York: Free Press, 1978.

Wasser, E. *Creative Approaches in Casework With the Aged.* New York: Family Service Association, 1966.

Weg, R.B. Beyond babies and orgasm. In B. Hess (Ed.), *Growing Old in America.* New Brunswick: Transaction, 1976.

Weg, R.B. Physiology of aging. In P.S. Woodruff and J.E. Birren (Eds.), *Aging: Scientific Perspectives and Social Issues.* Monterey, CA: Brooks-Cole, 1983.

Weisman, A., *On Dying and Denying.* New York; Behavioral Publ., 1972.

Wolff, K. Depression and suicide in the geriatric patient. *Journal of American Geriatric Society,* 17:668–72, 1969.

Woodruff, D.S., and J.E. Birren (Eds.). *Aging, Scientific Perspective and Social Issues.* New York: Van Nostrand, Reinhold, 1975.

Zarit, S.H. *Aging and Mental Disorders.* New York: Free Press, 1980.

Zing, W.W. A self-rating depression scale. *Archives of General Psychiatry,* 12:63–70, 1965.

INDEX

A

Aging
    adaptation to, 16–17
    disengagement and, 9
    fear of, 115
    myths of, 3–4
    personality changes and, 8–10
    process of, 13–17
    sex and, 10–12
    stereotypes about, 3
Agism, 18–20
Alcoholism, 35
Alexander, F., 93
Allen, E., 33
Altholtz, J., 136
Alzheimer's disease, 22
Alzheimer Disease and Related Disorders Association, 146
Anxiety, 91, 94
Anxiety reaction, 34–35
Arteriosclerosis, 22
Assertion training, 92–93, 143–145
    role playing and, 143
    stages in, 143
    structure of, 144
    techniques of, 145
Assessment, 43–60
    physical, 44–46
    psychiatric, 46–50
    psychological, 46–50
    steps in, 44–48

B

Baldwin, B., 77
Bankhoff, E., 146
Beck, A., 47, 97, 99
Beck Depression Inventory, 105
Behavior modification, 89–95
Behavior rehearsal, 93–94
Behavior therapy, 59
    characteristics of, 89–90
    use of, 90
Behavioral change, 72
Bell, J., 112
Bender Visual Motor Gestalt Test, 47
Bradford, L., 14, 116
Brain disease, 21–22
Breed, W., 30
Brody, E., 149
Burgess, A., 82
Busse, E., 31
Butler, R., 53, 63, 173

C

Casework, 63–65
    individual, 63
    family, 64
    supportive, 65
Catharsis, 63
Client-centered counseling, 139
Cognitive mastery, 105
Cognitive rehearsal, 99
Cognitive therapy, 59, 95–102
    application of, 98–99
    base of, 96–97
    depression and, 97–98
    problem solving and, 100
    results of, 98
Community mental health, 156–159
Consumer Union Report, 11–12
Coping methods, 80–81
Counterphobia, 52
Crisis, 76–78
    maturational, 77
    resolution of, 76

Crisis intervention, 59, 76–87
    application of, 83
    characteristics of, 78–79
    contracting and, 81–83
    evaluation of, 85–87
    steps in, 78–81

D

Death, 161–165
    acceptance of, 165–166
    denial and, 163
    depression and, 165
    fear of, 161–162
    responses to, 163–165
Delirium, 21
Dementia, 21–22
Dengrove, E., 94
Denial, 51–52
Depression, 50–52, 72–73, 181
    assessment of, 28–29
    characteristics of, 24
    diagnosis of, 45, 53
    disguised, 25–26
    electroconvulsive therapy and, 27
    features of, 23–24
    late life, 27–28
    medical disease and, 26
    severe, 24
    treatment of, 26–27
Disengagement, 9–10
Distancing, 107
Drug abuse, 35–36
Dying, 170–173
    coping with, 180–186
    fear of, 170
    grief and, 173–174
    life review and, 173
    terminal illness and, 172–173
Dying Patient's Bill of Rights, 171

E

Edinburg, M., 66
Emotional stress, 72
Epstein, L., 67, 74
Erikson, E., 16, 67, 106

F

Family Interaction Center, 112
Family relationships, 55
Family therapy, 60, 111–115
    application of, 113
    communication in, 115
    conflict resolution and, 113–114
    goals of, 112
Fischer, J., 95
Fixation, 52
Frey, P., 142
Functionalistic Ethics, 106

G

Garber, R., 153
Garrison, J., 91
Goalessness, 15, 117
Gottesman, L., 154
Gray Panthers, 19
Group psychotherapy, 136–138
    goals of, 137
    group compositions and, 136
    leadership in, 137
    purpose of, 136
Group therapy, 66, 129–147
    approaches to, 135
    confrontation in, 134
    contracting and, 131
    group leader's task in, 132
    planning and, 131
    purpose of, 129
    strategies in, 133

H

Haley, J., 112
Harris, M., 79
Herr, J., 112
Hospice care, 154–156
Housing, 17–18
Humanistic group therapy, 138–140
    client-centered approach and, 139
    growth groups and, 139
    purpose of, 138
    techniques of, 139–140
Hussian, R., 44, 92
Hyman, K., 115

Hypochondriasis, 30–32

I

Idealization, 52
Integrative counseling, 102–109
    assessment and, 105
    components of, 104
    morale and, 104
    steps in, 103
    theoretical base of, 105
Intelligence, 7–8
Interpersonal relations, 70
Instrumental values, 107–108

K

Kaplan, H., 121
Kardener, S., 78, 81
Kay, D., 38
Kent EGY Test, 46, 48
Koff, T., 156
Kubler-Ross, E., 165, 170
Kuhn, M., 19
Kurnat, J., 141

L

Lawton, M., 50
Levinson, H., 82
Life review, 107, 142
Life satisfaction, 105–106
Life styles, 12–14
Long-term care, 149–157
    milieu therapy and, 153
    problems in, 156–157
    remotivation and, 152
    therapeutic programs and, 151–154
Lowenthal, M., 12
Lowy, L., 18

M

McMahon, A., 140
McNulty, E., 154
Marlowe, R., 150
Marriage counseling, 115–120
    application of, 120
    problem solving and, 118–119

    retirement and, 117
Maslow, A., 14, 139
Masters, W., 125
Mattison, 141, 177
Memory loss, 8
Milieu therapy, 153
Minnesota Multiple Personality Inventory, 49
Mourning, 173–174
    anticipatory grief and, 178
    counseling and, 175
    depression and, 174
    grief and, 178
    guilt and, 174

O

OARS Mental Health Scale, 46
O'Leary, 89

P

Paranoid states, 32–34
Parkinson's disease, 22
Peck, R., 15
Perlman, H., 62
Perls, F., 139
Philadelphia Geriatric Center, 47
Physical examination, 44–46
Poggi, R., 137
Post, F., 33, 38
Poverty, 17, 18, 73
Problem solving, 100–102
    application of, 101
    cognitive therapy and, 100
    marriage counseling and, 118
    orientation to, 100
    steps in, 118
Projection, 52
Protective services, 63–64
Psychological tests, 46–50
Psychopathology, 77

R

Reality orientation, 151
Regression, 52
Reid, W., 67, 74
Relocation problems, 150
Reminiscing therapy, 140–142

Remotivational therapy, 152
Retirement, 12-15, 117
   adjustment to, 12-14
   loss of status and, 14-15
Ritualistic behavior, 52
Rogers, C., 139
Rorschock Inkblot test, 48
Ryden, M., 142

S

Satire, V., 112
Saunders, C., 167, 178
Schaie, K., 7
Self-help groups, 146-147
Semantic Differential Test, 106
Senior Actualization and Growth Experience, 140
Sex therapy, 124-126
   communication and, 123, 125
   sensate focusing and, 125
   techniques of, 124-126
Sexual dysfunctioning, 36-38
   causes of, 36
   therapy for, 37-38
Sexual functioning, 124-127
   aging and, 10-12
   body image and, 11
   changes in, 127
   decline in, 11
   difficulties in, 13
   health and, 126
   variation in, 11
Sexual impotence, 121, 122
   causes of, 122-123
   psychogenic blocking and, 125
   treatment of, 125
Sexual problems, 120-124
   aging and, 121
   attitudes and, 121
Sherman, E., 67, 102, 105, 106, 109
Short Portable Mental Status Questionnaire, 46
Silverstone, B., 115
Social casework, 61-62
   acceptance and, 62
   concrete services and, 63
   goals of, 61-62
   reassurance and, 62
   supportive, 61-67
Social network, 54
Social relations, 70
Stress, 38-40
   causes of, 38
   treatment of, 39-40, 91-95
Stress inoculation, 91-95
Strieb, G., 16
Stroke, 22-23
Suicide, 25, 29-30
Supportive therapy, 59
Systematic desensitization, 90-91

T

Task-centered casework, 67-76
   application of, 70
   evaluation of, 73-74
   guided practice and, 69
   incentives and, 69
   limitations of, 74
   steps in, 67-70
   target problems in, 74
   tasks in, 68
Taulbee, L., 152
Terminal illness, 175-177
Tibbetts, C., 19
Tobin, S., 141
Turner, F., 66

V

Value clarification, 104-105

W

Weakland, J., 112
Wechsler Adult Intelligence Scale, 48
Weg, R., 6, 127
Weisman, A., 168, 169
Widowed Persons Service, 146

Z

Zung, W., 47
Zung Self-Rated Depression Scale, 47